Discovering Ezekiel & Daniel

THE GUIDEPOSTS BIBLE STUDY PROGRAM

Floyd W. Thatcher   *General Editor*
Robin White Goode   *Associate Editor*
Bob E. Patterson   *Technical Consultant*

Ezekiel & Daniel

Discovering Ezekiel & Daniel	Bob E. Patterson
What This Scripture Means to Me	Jackie Stanley
Cover Artist	Ben Wohlberg
Maps	Dennis Hill

DISCOVERING EZEKIEL & DANIEL

The Guideposts Bible Study Program

GUIDEPOSTS®

Carmel   New York   10512

The photographs on the pages below were reproduced with the permission of the following photographers:
Louise Kohl Smith: 19 (*left and right*), 63, 75, 119, 146, 166, 177
Bruce Cresson: 43 (*top and bottom*), 53
Janet Shaffer: 88 (*left and right*)

THE GUIDEPOSTS BIBLE STUDY PROGRAM
The Books of Ezekiel & Daniel

Contents

Publisher's Introduction to Ezekiel

To the late-twentieth-century reader the Book of Ezekiel is difficult to understand and more than a little bewildering. Yet, it contains a powerful message for the people of God in any century, including our own.

The setting for the Book of Ezekiel is in one of the most creative periods of history. And the author is generally conceded to be the prophet Ezekiel himself—an enigmatic man, the son of a priest and most likely a priest himself. He was born in Palestine and probably grew up in Jerusalem. In 597 B.C. Nebuchadnezzar conquered Jerusalem and deported the intelligentsia to Babylon. Ezekiel was among this group and is thought to have been about twenty-five years old at the time.

We're told that Ezekiel was a happily married man, but his wife died at an early age. Five years after his arrival in Babylon, Ezekiel received his call to be a prophet of God (593 B.C.), a ministry he exercised until around 571 B.C. We learn from his writing that Ezekiel possessed a broad knowledge of the geography and culture of the times in which he lived and that he had a keen understanding of Hebrew history.

As a writer, Ezekiel's prose is quite labored at times, but he possessed a brilliant poetic sense. He was a master of metaphors and parables. He preached and wrote with a fiery zeal that at times is overwhelming.

We're told that during his life in exile Ezekiel lived

in his own home which was on or near the Chebar River, thought to be located between Babylon and Nippur. These exiles were granted considerable freedom and were allowed to pursue their vocations and live in peace. They were, however, restricted to Babylonia.

Ezekiel's message was directed toward the Jews in exile as well as to his countrymen left behind in Judah. The fact that he is so intimately acquainted with circumstances and events in Judah has caused some interpreters to speculate that he spent time there after his first deportation. However, that does not seem likely. We do know that messengers were permitted to travel back and forth between Judah and Babylon. This most likely accounted for the ready exchange of news and was the vehicle used for getting Ezekiel's messages across the miles to the Jews in Judah.

The primary message of the Book of Ezekiel is as up-to-date as if it had been written yesterday. The prophet wanted his listeners and readers in all of time to see God as the creative Force in all of life and to recognize Him as the Lord of history. And he issues the ringing call for them to worship the Lord and be His people and demonstrate before the world the majesty and holiness of the Lord. Central to all of this are these words given to Ezekiel by the Lord, "Therefore say unto the house of Israel, Thus saith the Lord God; I do not this for your sakes, O house of Israel, but for mine holy name's sake, which ye have profaned among the heathen [the nations], whither ye went. And I will sanctify my great name, which was profaned among the heathen [the nations], which ye have profaned in the midst of them; *and the heathen* [the nations] *shall know that I am the Lord,* saith the Lord God, when I shall be sanctified in you before their eyes [they will see me through you]" (36:22–23, italics mine).

Ezekiel's appeal is for the people of God to live each twenty-four-hour day in a way that others will see Him in and through us in the practical routines of life.

Preface to Ezekiel

All Bible students know how tough Ezekiel is to read, and how rewarding he is if we will stick with him long enough to understand. None of us can grasp all that God has to tell us through Ezekiel, but each of us can be enriched enormously by bringing away something from this study. Ezekiel gives us insights into the nature of God like few other prophets. He makes it clear that we stand in the presence of a holy God who will not tolerate evil, but by His power, even though we have fallen into sin, we can rise again.

Ezekiel is like the other Old Testament prophets in that he underscores the same seven themes that are in their messages: first, there is one God of the entire universe; second, morality is absolute and not relative; third, the messianic vision offers hope for a better tomorrow; fourth, much of the distress in the world is caused by false prophets; fifth, Israel (Judah) is God's avenue for ushering in peace and justice; sixth, knowledge of God comes from within; and seventh, the voice of authority is most likely not the voice of God.

Again, Ezekiel is the same as his fellow prophets

Like the Other Prophets

in that he saw God's Word as a distinct reality (almost as something material) that has an indescribably effective power on us like rain water on dry ground (Isa. 55:10–11). God's Word was more than word to the prophets; it was an action that set in motion the content of the message—God's power exploded through the prophet's voice like a balloon bursting. God's Word was God's Word, and not the prophet's. This simply meant that the prophet's authority was founded only in the Word of God he proclaimed.

Again Ezekiel is like the other prophets in that he was called by God to speak for God. Not only was Ezekiel's message *from* God, it was *about* God, His will, His covenant, His judgment and mercy, and His coming kingdom. As with Amos (Amos 4:12), Ezekiel was trying to make God the most genuine reality his listeners could know and experience.

Further, Ezekiel (like the other prophets) preached to the people of his own time and to their present situation. Ezekiel lists precise dates fourteen times, so we know that he was speaking to the people then and there. But along with this *forthtelling* for his own day, Ezekiel was *foretelling* for future times.

This doesn't mean that Ezekiel was forecasting events for the twenty-first century, or writing a history in advance. (Unfortunately, some Bible students try to join bits and prices of Ezekiel and the other prophets in order to shape a coherent picture of the "Last Days.")

When I look through a telescope in the Rocky Mountains, for example, it strikes me that one peak rises up right behind the other, when in reality they are miles apart. So when Ezekiel speaks about the coming of God the King and His kingdom, he puts his message in culturally conditioned forms (he talks about traveling in chariots, not Cadillacs), he was trying to get a response from his hearers (if they continued their rebellion against God, Jerusalem would be destroyed), and his forecasts about judgment were conditional (if his contemporaries repented of their evil ways, judgment would not come). Ezekiel's message to his fellow exiles in

Babylon about God's universal and coming kingdom was meant to guide and encourage his hearers, to serve as beacons for God's people to get their bearing and get out of Babylonian captivity.

Unlike the Other Prophets

On the other hand, there are ways in which Ezekiel is not like the other Old Testament prophets. We quickly and easily see how he is like them, but we are puzzled over his differences from them. His use of language, symbol, image, and metaphor unsettle our minds. It is not a simple task to get at the meaning of his vitally gripping allegories and word pictures. We, with our scientific and literal minds, need the sensitive imagination of the poet or the feeling of the traditional American spirituals ("wheels going round" and "dem dry bones") to open up Ezekiel's meaning. We do not always know why Ezekiel chose to use the literary forms that he did, so sometimes it is difficult for us to see the purpose behind his graphic images and to distinguish between the medium and the message. He uses more diversity in his mode of preaching than any other prophet.

Ezekiel's sermons were never simple preaching; he told about visions, gave allegories and parables, and quoted poetry—all of which were full of hidden symbols and meaning. He sometimes acted out (pantomimed) his messages like a drama coach. His symbolism is the richest of any of the prophets.

Furthermore, Ezekiel was a strange personality and would have been an odd sort of fellow in any culture, ancient or modern. Some Bible students have even doubted if he was fully sane at all times, or if his elevator always got to the top floor. Certainly his psychic peculiarities would make a fascinating psychological study, but his unusual temperament throws more light on the *form* of his message than upon its *content.*

Neither his character nor experiences were ordinary run-of-the-mill types, but there is no reason to question his sanity. He was an unusually gifted genius, and turned his extraordinary imagination to speaking God's message to a conquered people through images of immense evocative power.

The Man and His Times

Ezekiel was the right man, with the right message, at the right time. He watched his nation die and crawl into exile where he became its pastor, looking for a hopeful message amid the ruins. He was like the Christian Kagawa in his beloved Japan after the A-bomb destroyed Hiroshima and Nagasaki. Ezekiel saw the destruction of Judah as the judgment of God, but he longed for the recovery and restoration of his countrymen. He resolved that Judah should rise and live again, but this time with a new kind of national integrity. He pictured the nation of Judah as a valley of dry bones and raised the question, "Can these bones live again?"

The Book of Ezekiel is simply outlined and we will follow his four divisions in our first four lessons. As a young priest Ezekiel was deported to Babylon in 597 B.C. with the first group of exiles, and five years later he received a call from God to be a prophet to his people. He first preached doom upon Judah (Chapters 1–24) and the surrounding neighboring nations (Chapters 25–32). Then in 587 B.C. Jerusalem was sacked and sent up in smoke, and Ezekiel's ministry took on a new direction. He replaced judgment with a vision of God's people rehabilitated, reunited, and restored. He held out a new future in the Holy Land for the new group of exiles (Chapters 35–39). In the last section of his book (Chapters 40–48) he pictures, in a highly symbolic manner and in a spirit of ecstasy, the Judeans back at home in Jerusalem with an ideal Temple from which life would flow out and bless the whole land. The religion of the Hebrews had not come to an end—there was hope for the future.

To get into the Book of Ezekiel we need to turn back to 597 B.C., the year that King Nebuchadnezzar deported the first group of Jews to Babylon. Ezekiel was in this early group of exiles (1:2) that were the cream of the population. Nebuchadnezzar deported three groups to hold as hostages—the royal family, the wealthy landed gentry, and the priestly class. Only the poorest people were left behind. We can assume, then, that Ezekiel belonged to the aristocracy of Jerusalem and probably to the powerful priesthood of Zadok, the High Priest installed by Solomon.

A thousand miles from home, he settled by the banks of the river Chebar with his fellow exiles. Chebar was a large irrigation canal that piped water from the river Euphrates through Nippur, a city that lay a short distance southeast of Babylon. The ruins of Babylon are still dimly visible to us today, and it is likely that Ezekiel visited it in its glory. Five years after his deportation (c. 593 B.C.) he received his call to prophesy in the village of Tel-Abib, a small town built on the edge of the canal. For the next twenty years he served the exiles as pastor, counselor, prophet, and priest. Because of Ezekiel, "These bones did live again."

Ezekiel For Our Day

Ezekiel spoke to the people of his time certainly, but his words have an ongoing character that can help us today. He revealed part of God's purpose then which is still capable of achieving a greater fullness in us, so that when it is *filled full* it is *fulfilled.* The question is, how can we listen to Ezekiel preach relevantly to a group of people twenty-five hundred years ago and still apply it meaningfully to our lives today? God's Word for His people then was "Love the Lord your God and love your neighbor," and His Word today is generally the same. Sins for Ezekiel are still sins for Christians, and God's love and holiness for Israel still hold for the church. The faithful covenant God of 587 B.C. is the same yesterday, today, and forever.

The Book of Ezekiel can be vital for us today if we ask, "What was Ezekiel saying that was true then (that is always true for all people), and what in his message is true now, for me, in my very particular situation?" Just as there was a "then" for Ezekiel's hearers, there is also a "now" for us. Jesus grew up reading the Book of Ezekiel as a part of His Bible. And we too can read these messages as a part of God's inspired word to us, and be a better people because of his message. It is possible to study Ezekiel and come "to see Jesus Christ more clearly, to love Him more dearly, and to follow Him more nearly."

Chronological Outline

Date	Event
640 B.C.	Accession of King Josiah
627 B.C.	Josiah begins his reform
626 B.C.	The call of Jeremiah
623 B.C.	Ezekiel born
622 B.C.	The book of the Law found in the Temple
609 B.C.	Josiah is killed at Megiddo; the accession of Johoiahaz, and of Jehoiakim three months later
605 B.C.	Assyria is destroyed by Babylon
598 B.C.	Babylon attacks Judah; Jehoiakim dies; the accession of Jehoiachin
597 B.C.	Jehoiachin surrenders to Babylon and is deported; the accession of Zedekiah; 26-year-old Ezekiel goes into exile
593 B.C.	Ezekiel receives his call to prophesy
588 B.C.	Babylon besieges Jerusalem; Ezekiel's wife dies
587 B.C.	Jerusalem is captured and the Temple is destroyed; Zedekiah and the people are deported; Gedaliah is appointed governor
582 B.C. (?)	Gedaliah is assassinated; Jeremiah in Egypt
573 B.C.	Ezekiel's vision of the Temple; his last recorded prophecy

LESSON 1
Ezekiel 1–19

Prophecies of Doom to the Exiles Before the Fall of Jerusalem

Holy Lord, Help me to listen for Your voice as You speak to me through this lesson. AMEN.

On July 31, 593 B.C. the thirty-year-old Ezekiel, trained as a priest, suddenly had to switch vocations and become a prophet. Let's see how this happened, how he responded, and what this can say to *us*.

Ezekiel was born about 623 B.C., probably in Jerusalem, where his influential father, Buzi, was an important priest serving in the great Temple (1:1–3). Ezekiel was being trained to follow in his father's footsteps, but this was not to be. Jerusalem was coming apart at the seams. When Ezekiel was twenty-six years old (597 B.C.), Jerusalem was attacked by the supreme military power of the time, Babylon. Nebuchadnezzar (also spelled Nebuchadrezzar) the Babylonian emperor carried off as hostages Jerusalem's key citizens and families to live as exiles in a region that is now part of Iraq. Judah as a state survived after a fashion for ten more years (until 587 B.C.), but its destruction was inevitable. Ezekiel and the other exiles settled in and built for themselves mud brick houses along the irrigation canal Chebar a few miles

Ezekiel's Vision and Call (1:1–3:27)

I Was Among the Captives

south of the capital city of Babylon in a village called Tel-Abib.

For Ezekiel "life had caved in, so what then?" He had been jerked up from a privileged position in the cool highlands of Jerusalem and dumped in the damp humid plains around Babylon to work the wastelands for foreigners. He was trained to enter the priesthood at thirty, but the grim reality was that he was grubbing for a living as an exile in a strange land on his thirtieth birthday.

Frustrated, humiliated, and grinding out an existence, of what use was his priestly education now? Others have cracked under such pressure, but he hung on and hoped. Although born to be a priest, God turned him into one of the most significant prophets of all history. Young, disappointed, and cut off from his calling, he learned something of how God works in our lives. Even in a wasteland, God still has something for us to do. A new vocation from God can in itself revive our hope, give us a new direction, and restore our vision.

If God doesn't give up on us, we shouldn't give up on Him. A young man lost his girlfriend and in despair was about to jump from a Mississippi River bridge to his death. He changed his mind and instead returned to his room and wrote the words to a song. That song, "Good Night, Irene," became a popular hit during the 1950s and earned its writer a fortune. Martin Luther King, Jr. used this event in a sermon on hope and drove home the point, "Don't jump! Don't jump! God still has a remarkable future for you." Ezekiel didn't jump, and neither should we.

Ezekiel's Vision

Ezekiel started by watching an approaching thunderstorm and ended with a stunning heavenly vision of God (1:4–28). Central to the vision are a heavenly chariot, living creatures, and a life-giving Spirit. The chariot was the mobile throne of God which could go wherever it wanted to go with omni-directional mobility. The wheels were full of eyes which symbolized God's power to see all that goes on in the world. Nothing in Ezekiel's religious training had prepared him for this picture of God, and he was so stunned that he was knocked to the ground. He discovered that his previous ideas of God were too small and that the living God was totally beyond his comprehension. God was not limited to the Temple in Jerusalem or even the land of Palestine, but was sovereign and omniscient everywhere. God is not restricted by anything, and this new idea totally overwhelmed Ezekiel.

I live in Waco, Texas, situated on the Brazos River, and teach at Baylor University. Sometimes Baylor is jokingly referred to as the "Jerusalem on the Brazos." But that expression must remain a bit of humor, because God is not confined to a particular place, church, city, or country. To be away from the Brazos is not to be away from God.

The four faces of the living creatures in Ezekiel's vision—a man, an ox, an eagle, and lion—represented the major areas of created life and symbolized the fact that God is the Lord of nature. Nothing can finally separate us from God's care or concern (Rom. 8:38–39). The famous American psychologist, Antoine Boisen, said that in his own emotional illness and at the depths of his psychosis, he sensed the presence of God tugging him back toward wholeness and mental stability.

The speech-defying figure of God seated on the great sapphire rainbow was a crucial vision and probably saved the faith of the Hebrew exiles. With a destroyed homeland a thousand miles to the west, they might have assumed that God Himself had been destroyed. This vision retaught Ezekiel and the exiles that God still rode upon His chariot wherever He willed in His creation, not only seeing all events in history but controlling them as well. Ezekiel's vision illustrates the sixth of the common themes of the prophets—knowledge of God comes from within.

Knocked flat to the ground by the awesome majesty and holiness of God, Ezekiel was given no time to indulge in his mystical experience of finite dependence before God's infinite power and glory (2:1–7). God promptly ordered him to his feet and gave him a set of marching orders. God said to him, "Son of man" (the equivalent of "a mortal human being" in contrast to God's lofty being) you are to be "a prophet among them" (2:3–5).

God's Call To Change Vocations

Ezekiel's call from God gives us a clue to our own call. God called him; he didn't call himself to be a prophet. Without God's initiative, neither Ezekiel nor we have the strength to do the job. Again, he was to speak God's Word, not his own. You and I are called to correctly interpret and apply the Bible, the equivalent of the spoken word in Ezekiel's ministry. Third, he was not to be discouraged by the lack of immediate success. You and I are called to be faithful to our mission in the face of frightening circumstances and leave the results to God and later history. The success of our witness and service depends on God's will and not our skill. Finally, God is flexible, and can change the arena of our activity for Him in the middle of our career. God shifted Ezekiel from the priestly to the prophetic path as circumstances changed.

I once spent a Sunday afternoon with a Christian lady talking about her call to be a foreign missionary. She trained well for the task, but many things blocked her way. She wasn't flexible enough to see that God could use her equally well at home, so she had spent two decades in depression, frustration, guilt, and uselessness in her home state. She was miserable and made her family miserable. A careful reading of the Book of Ezekiel would have shown her that our gracious God can use us in another field of labor if we can't make it into the first field.

An Ordination Service for the Prophet

God next commanded the young man to eat "a roll of a book" (a scroll) whose words were full of "lamentations, and mourning, and woe" (2:8–3:3). In other words, when Ezekiel spoke to the exiles, they would hear his words with misery. Since the people were rebellious and apostate, his message of truth and joy would make the ungodly mournful.

The prophet's obedience to God made the people's disobedience stand out boldly in all its ugliness and distastefulness. An honest word makes a liar uncomfortable. The lesson for us is that our obedience to God may cause others pain, and in their anger and guilt they may inflict pain on us. But God's will, "as honey for sweetness," is the very food that will give us the strength to carry out

Pictured here are two views of the Ishtar Gate, a principal entryway to the city of Babylon. The gate was named after the goddess Ishtar who was worshiped in Mesopotamia from the earliest times to approximately the second and first centuries B.C. Ishtar was considered both a goddess of war and a fertility goddess. Since Ezekiel's home in Babylonia was in Tel-Abib, just a short distance south of Babylon, he would have been very aware of the Ishtar cult.

His purposes, God's call to a tough task doesn't really catch us by surprise. Dietrich Bonhoeffer, the Christian martyr of a German concentration camp in the Second World War, said, "Discipleship means allegiance to the suffering Christ." Great leaders have always demanded our best efforts. Sir Winston Churchill's rousing speech in the English

House of Commons on May 13, 1940, is best remembered by the grim words, "I have nothing to offer but blood, toil, tears, and sweat."

The Vocation of Tough Love

God told Ezekiel that the exiles were "impudent and hard-hearted . . . a rebellious house," but promised to make him as hard as flint and equal to the task of speaking before willful rebellion (3:7–9). The name *Ezekiel* means "God hardens," and apparently the young man was too sensitive, tender hearted, romantic, and sentimental to be a prophet. God promised to make him like Himself, a God of "tough love" who cared for His people so much that He endured the agony and pain that it cost Him to bring a hard message (3:4–15). It would have been unloving of God not to try to rescue His people from their rebellion. Remember, it is a privilege to suffer for "Christ's sake," because in so doing we share in the suffering of God Himself. God is love, and one side of His love is agony and pain.

At first Ezekiel's task seemed so unkind to his friends in exile that it made him bitter, but as he continued to listen to God, the message became part of his very being. He sat among his friends for a week, silent and astonished, and then he took up his work as a prophet.

His Personal Responsibility: A Watchman

Ezekiel, in near-shock, reflected on God's vision and his own call to a prophetic ministry (3:16–27). This was only the beginning, for God's Word came to him forty-nine more times. Now we read that on the eighth day God's Word came again, and laid on him a heavy personal responsibility: He was to be "a watchman unto the house of Israel" (3:17). He suddenly found himself responsible for sentry duty over his friends in exile, and like it or not, he could never again think of only his own likes or wishes. In the same way, you and I can never separate our Christian vocation and our guardianship over others. Privilege brings responsibility, and when we learn to love as deeply as God loves, the responsibility can become a joyful privilege.

Daniel Webster, America's Secretary of State many years ago, was once asked to tell what was the most important thought he had ever had. Following a brief silence, he confidently replied, "That of my individual responsibility to God."

God then told Ezekiel to go back to the "plain" (the southern Tigris-Euphrates river valley) for a while and receive further instructions (3:22). He was to be God's *spokesman,* yes, but there were times in the future when he was to keep his mouth shut. And like Ezekiel, we too are totally at God's command in our Christian vocation. We must remain close enough to God to catch His signals about when we are to speak and when we are not to speak.

Let's keep in mind that when a prophet's message went beyond the power of words to express, he turned to actions that were louder than words (e.g. Isa. 20:1–2; Jer. 19, 27:1–28:16). The Book of Ezekiel swarms with dramatic acts, and in this section the prophet turns to drama and demonstrations to describe the siege of Jerusalem and the exile to follow.

Ezekiel was told to take a "tile" (a flat, wet, clay brick of the type used in many houses in Tel-Abib), draw a map of Jerusalem on it, pretend the map was the city, and pretending that he was God, carry on a miniature siege of the city (4:1–3). Second, after the mock siege, he was instructed to lie for some time each day for three-hundred and ninety days on one side (with arms bare and bound) to show the length of Israel's captivity, and forty days for Judah's captivity. He probably repeated this symbolic act every day outside his own house (4:4–8). Third, he was to depict the hunger and thirst of the people under the siege by the scarcity of food and water that he ate and drank daily (4:9–17).

Ezekiel's actions turned out to be more forceful than a sermon, and quickly caught the attention of the exiles. These prisoners-of-war soon concluded that Ezekiel was telling them that God in judgment was determined that their beloved city, Jerusalem, would be destroyed. Therefore, they could not look to the people left behind in Jerusalem to rescue them from Babylon. The city had starved for spiritual food for many years, now it would starve for physical

Visions and Oracles of Judgment on Jerusalem (4:1–7:27)

Symbolic Siege of Jerusalem

food. Turning from evil and turning to God in repentance was their only source of hope.

For fourteen months Ezekiel kept up this mock siege, and no doubt endured the jeering of the crowd that gathered daily to watch him. But the days of acting out this painful pantomime were finally over, and, if the people had been reflective, they would have taken heart at the promise that God can turn darkness into light and doom into hope.

One significant event in this acted-out sermon tells us something precious about the character of God. Ezekiel reacted in horror when God told him to bake his bread in a fire of human dung, so God let him substitute cattle manure for cooking fuel (4:12–13). Ezekiel wasn't just being fussy—because of his priestly training he looked upon human excrement as violating the purity required in his relationship to God (Deut. 23:12–14). God is not unfeeling about our tender consciences, and in this instance He kindly changed His original order. Some of the force of the original symbolism was lost, and yet God trimmed the message to better suit the disposition of the messenger. Serving God may entail suffering, but God in His love for us makes it as easy for us as He can.

Complete Desolation: the Shearing of Jerusalem

God next told Ezekiel to shave himself until he became bald and beardless. Then he was to collect the hair and destroy it by burning, cutting with the sword, and scattering to the wind (5:1–2). A shaved head was a mark of captivity to the Hebrews, a sign of shame and deep mourning.

Ezekiel then interpreted the meaning of his symbolic act for the gathering crowd (5:3–17). He said that one third of Jerusalem's citizens would die in the coming siege, one third would die in defense of the city, and one third would scatter after the city fell.

Ezekiel's actions were astonishingly eccentric, but by the grace of God abnormalities have produced some of history's notable personalities. Ezekiel's ecstatic and dramatic acts reinforced his words from God. His ability to identify himself with the exiles and then return to his normal everyday roles shows a sensitive soul caught in a dreadful time of history, driven by a burning zeal for God, and suffering deeply over the tragedy of his people. If God can use

Ezekiel with all of his personal peculiarities, then I find it consoling that God can also use me with my own set of strange behaviors. And if God can use me, He can use anybody.

Babylon was a problem for Jerusalem, but Jerusalem was its own worst problem. The people of the city had rejected God, so God had rejected them. God had given the city much, but the people had squandered their opportunities to be a guiding light to the neighboring nations. In the Preface we noted that the fifth theme shared in common by all the prophets was that Israel is God's avenue for ushering in peace and justice. As Christians we are God's temples (1 Cor. 3:16), and from us much is to be expected (Luke 12:48). God loves us deeply, and we are responsible to Him. Yes, God loves us deeply, and in that lies our hope and joy.

God's actions toward His chosen people were designed to show the gentile nations His true nature (Gen. 22:18; Exod. 19:6). But since Israel and Judah had refused to cooperate with God by failing to do the things God called them into existence to do, that for which they had been called into existence, He would use their failure to show the world His integrity and justice. Similarly, if we don't voluntarily honor God through our pleasures, we will involuntarily honor Him through our pain. The irony is that God's message will be proclaimed even if we as messengers fail.

Pagan Idolatry Condemned

Having spoken against the city of Jerusalem, Ezekiel now turned to "the mountains of Israel," a figure of speech for *high places* (funerary cairns used as open-air pagan sanctuaries) (6:2). Here the chosen people worshiped fertility goddesses such as Ashera and Anath. The first theme that all the prophets preached was that there is only one God of the entire universe. But it was this old and false faith on the hillsides that had come into vogue and caused the true faith to decline throughout the land. Ezekiel promised that it would be destroyed along with every other corrupt phase of life in Judah (6:1–14). To worship God's creation in any form was a disservice to the Creator.

Then comes the promise: a "remnant" would survive and "remember me," the true God, "among the nations," and return to the foundations of their faith (6:8–9). Sorrow over past sins can be a teaching tool that God uses to bring us back to Himself. In the New Testament, Judas Iscariot was horrified over his betrayal of Jesus, and in despair he killed himself. Simon Peter was also horrified over his denial of Jesus, but he soon repented and was restored as a leader of the band of disciples. God left it up to Judah to make the decision to live or die, just as He gave to Judas and Peter the choice to repent or not. God wills only love for us, but we have the freedom to reject Him and His love.

National Pride Leads to National Ruin

Ezekiel's urgent theme here is "The End" of the homeland (7:1–27). Judah's national character of pomposity and pride had come into full bloom. The people had turned against God so God turned against them; the people had not accepted God's covenant love so now God would come to them as an enemy. We will see Ezekiel return to this theme of national arrogance again and again.

God's gifts to the homeland should have made the people of Judah grateful and humble, but instead they swelled up in pride at their own pre-eminence. When "the end" came, they would rush to their three standbys to rescue them—their army, their wealth, and "their" Temple. The army, though, was a false security: "but none goeth to the battle." Their financial support couldn't buy them out of their mess: "They shall cast their silver in the streets." And their long-neglected Temple would not save them: "their holy places shall be defiled." Their three false faiths had invited disaster, and their pride went before their fall.

Visions of Jerusalem and Its Final Fall (8:1–11:25)

In September, 592 B.C., fourteen months after his initial chariot vision in the plain, (chapter 1), Ezekiel received an extraordinarily powerful vision of the idolatry going on in the Temple in Jerusalem and the destruction of the city itself.

Pagan Gods in God's House

By this time "the elders of Judah" had come to recognize Ezekiel as a prophet, and they were visiting him in his home to get his opinion about the fate of their beloved Jerusalem. During their visit God gave him a vivid vision of Jerusalem (8:1–18). Ezekiel said that God "took me by a lock of mine head; and the spirit lifted me up between the earth and the heaven, and brought me in the visions of God to Jerusalem, to the door of the inner gate, that looketh toward the north; where was the seat of the image of jealousy" (or "lust") (8:3).

He saw in his dream that an image of the pagan fertility goddess Ashera had been set up in God's Temple in Jerusalem (2 Kings 21:7), and this Canaanite goddess of lust was driving God from His own house. The first of the ten commandments was being broken, and God was sadly being displaced by a false presence. And once God left the Temple, there was no power to prevent its destruction. The people had forgotten entirely the reason for the Temple's existence.

Next, in his dream, Ezekiel discovered an underground secret room where seventy of Jerusalem's citizens were burning incense to false gods. The walls of this frescoed room were covered with inanimate murals of unclean or "unkosher" creatures forbidden in the diet of the chosen people (8:7–13). The elders were probably still publicly loyal to God but were secretly involved in debauched worship. They felt that God had forsaken them ("the Lord hath forsaken the earth"), and they were free to turn to other gods. These leaders had lost their faith in God, and this accounted for the spiritual decline of the nation. When leaders lose their integrity, the people pay the consequences. From now on, God would turn to the elders in Ezekiel's house to lead the exiles. The "sin of all sins" is the distrust of God.

To add to the seventy elders' new idolatry, "there sat women weeping for Tammuz" (8:14). Tammuz was a Babylonian god of vegetation and the underworld. He was also the husband-lover of the goddess Ishtar, and ritual weeping and debased orgies were a part of his worship. At the entrance to God's sanctuary the women wept for a dying god. In this kind of atmosphere, how could God stay in Jerusalem?

Ezekiel ended his visionary tour of the Temple in

the inner "holy of holies" where he found twenty-five men as "they worshipped the sun toward the east" (8:16). The people of Judah had worshiped everything but the true God, and consequently had lost their way. Failing in their faith in God, they turned on each other in violence. The only solid foundation for good moral conduct is a good relationship with God. As the Russian novelist Dostoevski said, "If God is dead, anything is permissible."

Death Squads Slaughter the City

Then, Ezekiel saw divine executioners killing those who had pledged loyalty to God but who had secretly worshiped other gods (9:1–11). For the first time in the Old Testament we see a well-developed superhistorical (apocalyptic) description of God's judgment. Usually God's judgment was carried out in the regular processes of history, but it is different in Ezekiel. (We will see this sort of description become quite common in the Book of Daniel.) Since guilt had its deepest roots in the Temple, that's where the death squads began their slaughter (9:6). What had started in Egypt in love seven hundred years before (the Exodus) now ends in a bloodbath of the chosen people. Only by the mercy of God would a remnant remain alive to carry out God's greater purpose for the world.

The Lord Leaves His Temple

Next, the prophet saw a supernatural (apocalyptic) figure of destruction dressed in linen take the fire of God from among the heavenly wheels and scatter it over the city. Then God prepared to leave the sanctuary of the Temple since it could no longer be His dwelling place (10:1–22). "Then the glory of the Lord departed from off the threshold of the house" (10:18).

Ezekiel used the expression "the glory of the Lord" nineteen times to highlight the objective overpowering majesty of God. He was keenly aware of God's sovereignty and of our sinful distance from Him. Ezekiel saw God clothed in light as a garment, dwelling in unapproachable splendor, ruling the world in unrivaled justice, and in whose presence evil could not stand. No other prophet emphasized the lofty superiority of God as did Ezekiel. God's "wholly otherness" was just an expression of what God was really like Himself.

This is an insight that we Christians can't be careless about. God is our loving Father, but He is also our Heavenly Parent. Jesus' favorite address for God in prayer was Holy Father. On the lips of Jesus "Holy" caught all the unapproachable majesty of Ezekiel's vision of God. The New Testament uniquely highlights God as Father, but never to the neglect of His holy loftiness. We are wise when we take both Ezekiel and Jesus seriously.

The people of Jerusalem had nothing to fear from God's purity as long as they were pure, but when they became unholy and corrupt, God's fire turned into hot coals of destruction. Purity spurned is destruction invited; God's holiness warms the devout but consumes the ungodly. And the absence of God is the worst horror of all. To be removed from God is the final state of hell. The tragedy of Jerusalem was that it ended up as dead as Sodom and Gomorrah (Gen. 19:24). God did not want to leave Jerusalem, but He was evicted by a people in the steadfast pursuit of evil. In Ezekiel's vision, God in His throne chariot paused a moment at the east gate (10:19) before forsaking the sanctuary that had been desecrated by pagan rites and superficial worship.

What a shock it must have been to the people of Jerusalem to wake up to the fact that God had deserted His own house. The medieval Christian monks used to say that there were going to be three surprises in heaven. First, that you were there. Second, that they were there. And third, that so many others were not there. As long as the citizens of Jerusalem continued their evil way, God would never be there. What a sad absence. Here Ezekiel is sounding the second prophetic theme that morality is absolute and not relative.

The End of False Optimism

Next Ezekiel saw in his vision twenty-five of the city's rulers assembled in a national council to review the progress of their work. They had effectively rebuilt the destruction of Nebuchadnezzar's first invasion (597 B.C.) and were smugly congratulating themselves. But in their rebuilding they had built God out of the picture, they had slain innocent citizens, and they had never raised the question as to why God had allowed the city to be destroyed the first time. By failing to recognize the moral decay behind their first disaster, they were in for a second disaster. God planned to reverse their pompous proverbs, and as if in anticipation of their judgment, one of the twenty-five, Pelatiah, suddenly dropped dead, possibly from a heart attack. Pelatiah's death was a foretaste of the much darker tragedy of the fall of the city of Jerusalem (11:1–25).

As Christians we may have to look at Pelatiah's death a long time before we can see any lessons in it for ourselves. But St. Augustine gave us a hint when he said that every man's inordinate affection is his own punishment. We can get so caught up in our own personal wishes that we leave God out. And God is such a Gentleman that He will let us have what we insist on having, and that is punishment in itself.

Ezekiel came from the sad vision of Jerusalem to the exiles in Tel-Abib with a beautiful and encouraging promise. Jerusalem may have written off the exiles, but God in a grand reversal had written off Jerusalem and turned to the exiles with the promise of a new exodus and the reestablishment of the faith in the promised land. God planned to use the exiles in a rebuilding program. They would have to undergo a fundamental change in nature before their future could brighten, but God said He would give them a new heart and a new spirit so that "they may walk in my statutes, and keep mine ordinances, and do them: and they shall be my people, and I will be their God" (11:20). Jerusalem in its grasping greed had lost its last opportunity, and a future for God's people now lay with the exiles.

Here Ezekiel echoes the third prophetic theme that there is, by the providence of God, a hope for a better tomorrow. As Christians we have every reason for hope because of what Christ has done for us. The Old Testament prophets tried to give some of this hope to their own people. When a famous tailor was asked to give the secret of his success he said, "Always put a knot in your thread." Ezekiel kept the exiles from coming unraveled by holding a bright future before them. None of the Old Testament saints could have imagined the hope that we as Christians hold in our hearts today when we address God in prayer as "Father." As false optimisms fade, we are opened up to true optimism by the grace of God.

At this point Ezekiel began a new phase in his life and ministry. He had to destroy the false optimism of the exiles at Tel-Abib that Jerusalem would survive—God could no longer live in that city—and he had to convince them that God had a future for them—God would now live with them.

For Ezekiel action always spoke louder than words—he would first show, dramatize, and then tell, interpret (12:1–20). By this time his neighbor exiles had become accustomed to his enacted parables. Now they saw him pack whatever goods an exile could carry, dig a hole in the wall of his house, and sneak out through the hole in the twilight. The next day he explained to them that this was about to happen to Jerusalem: "they shall remove and go into captivity" (12:11).

Historically, this is what happened to the ill-starred monarch Zedekiah who was brought bound and blinded to Babylon (2 Kings 25:4–7, Jer. 39:4–8; 52:7–11). If the people of Jerusalem could not hear God whispering to them in their pleasures, maybe they could hear him shouting in their pain. The pain of judgment is something that most of us as church people are too sentimental to think about, talk about, or preach about. But it can be one of God's tools to bring us to reality. Jonathan Edward's sermon on judgment, "Sinners in the Hands of an Angry God," pictured people being held over the pit of hell as a man might hold a spider over a fire, and pleaded with them to turn to the Lord before it was too late. We're told that people trembled and cried, and all of New England was transformed in the early 1700s. Edward's same tactics might not work for us today, but the sadness of his theme is always appropriate.

Ezekiel continued to act out the parable by eating

Prophecies About Jerusalem and Its Coming Fall (12:1–19:14)

A Parable of the Horrors of Life in Exile

a meal while pretending to be quaking in terror at the coming invasion. The leaders of the city had acted violently against their citizens, so they were to reap a harvest of violence—from now on they would eat their meals in despair (12:17–20). They would even choke on two of their favorite proverbs: judgment would not come, and even if it did it was still a generation away.

God condemned the popular notion that prophetic judgment could be ignored—the prophets are only crying "wolf"—and corrected the idea that destruction was far distant—after us the "deluge." Faith in God is either immediately relevant to a person's life, or it is not faith at all. They would have done better to heed another proverb, "Repent now, and avoid the rush later on."

Here a Christian might say, "I have nothing to learn about repentance, because I have already repented and been forgiven by God." But Martin Luther was more nearly correct when he said that we need to repent from the first day of our Christian lives until the last day of our lives. The Apostle Paul, at the end of a long and Godly life, humbly said that he was still the "chief of sinners." Jonathan Swift, English satirist and clergyman, said that we should never be ashamed to admit that we are in the wrong, for that is merely another way of saying that we are wiser today than we were yesterday. Repentance frees us to receive God's help.

False Prophets and Deceptive Daughters Described and Judged

God next told Ezekiel to speak against the "foolish prophets, that follow their own spirit, and have seen nothing," and He said there were three things wrong with the prophets who failed Jerusalem in its time of distress (13:1–23). First, they spoke out of their own minds and followed the inclinations of their own hearts, telling happy lies in the place of hard truths. A true prophet was the medium for God's Word, not his own. Second, in a crisis these false prophets fulfilled no function, but looked instead to their own comfort. A true prophet would have built a spiritual wall of defense around the city. Third, these "foolish prophets" deliberately lied and then expected God to back up their word to save Himself from embarrassment.

They mistook their hallucinations for the character of God. But a true prophet would never put an untruth on the lips of the divine. And because of their delusive visions and blasphemous attitudes these religious pirates were disinherited by God and fell down like a crumbling wall.

Counterfeit substitutes began to replace the false prophets. The women described in verses 17–23—soothsayers, witches, and sorceresses—had turned to magic arts as a source of power and money. People paid them to use their powers as a weapon to eliminate competition, to bend God's will to their own lust and hate, and to arrange events to suit their own greed. These women who disinherited the righteous and encouraged the wicked were condemned by God as were the false prophets.

And false prophets weren't around just in Old Testament times because Jesus warned against them in the New Testament church (Matt. 7:15–20). Jesus warned us to select our spiritual leaders with care. The basic fault of false leaders in the church is self-interest—leading or teaching solely for gain, prestige, or to transmit their own ideas. The false prophets of today, as in Ezekiel's time, are caught up solely in observing externals, in imposing prohibitions, and in being arrogantly separate. The fourth prophetic theme, that much of the distress in the world is caused by false prophets, is still true.

Religious Duplicity: the Veneer of Orthodoxy

When the elders of the exile met with Ezekiel, he delivered a message that was intended both for them and for Jerusalem: "Repent, and turn yourselves from your idols" (14:6). In an X-ray look into their hearts, Ezekiel knew that these religious leaders secretly looked for help other than from God to rescue them from exile (14:1–23). These spiritually schizophrenic elders, seeking a word from God while secretly harboring idols, couldn't see that it was idolatry that had landed them in exile. They must have thought God was blind. But God in His compassion couldn't leave them in their delusion, so He ordered them to do an "about face," to repent.

No doubt the fallacious rumor had been spread among the exiles (by the false prophets?) that God would spare Jerusalem because of the remnant of righteous people in it. But God quickly killed that false hope by saying that a nation that persists in sin will not escape from judgment even if three universal examples of righteousness live there. Not even the super-saints, Noah, Daniel, and Job, could halt God's judgment on a persistently evil nation. Noah is well known from the story of the Flood, while the Book of Job tells the story of the upright patriarch. Dan'el (so spelled in Ezekiel and not to be associated with the Book of Daniel which we will study in Lessons 5–8) was an ancient and good Canaanite sage.

But Jerusalem's doom was a prelude to a future renewal of a purified and obedient few. It would not work out all right for Jerusalem, but God wanted the remnant in the exile to still trust Him and accept His offer for life.

The Useless Vine and the Unfaithful Wife

Chapter 15 is built on an ancient allegory of the vine, a vine which is useless for purposes other than producing grapes. Even for fuel it is practically useless, and Ezekiel used this well-known figure for unproductive Judah which must be destroyed (15:1–16:63).

The people back in Jerusalem were beyond redemption or rescue. The sole function of the people of Judah was to convey God's love to the world. When they failed to fulfill this calling, they had no further reason for living. Here Ezekiel brought out the fifth theme of the prophets, namely, that the Hebrew people were God's means for ushering in justice and peace. If they failed in that, there was no longer a purpose for them to exist.

Chapter 16 is a parable applied to the people of Judah, depicting them as a wife unfaithful to her covenant position. The parable moves through seven stages. Stage one: Jerusalem, the foundling (16:1–7). Here Ezekiel calls into question the purity of Judah's origin which was the basis for its false national pride. Jerusalem's ancestry was pagan (Canaanite and Hittite) and not related to the covenant, so God's love for them was not influenced by their ancestry. God loved them while they were still unlovely, and they only grew lovely because God loved them.

Stage two: Jerusalem, the maiden queen (16:8–14). Jerusalem was adopted—by marriage—into God's covenant and transformed into a queen with all the royal trappings (the golden age of Solomon).

Stage three: Jerusalem, the degenerate (16:15–22). Instead of being faithful to God, Jerusalem trusted in her beauty and practiced harlotry with every passerby (the widespread cult prostitution of King Manasseh, 687–642 B.C.). Forgetting her dependence on God, she became pridefully obsessed with herself and fell into a life of lurid evil.

Stage four: Jerusalem, the condemned (16:23–24). It was idolatry at home and alliances abroad, where political treaties always led to religious syncretism, that led the city to degeneration. Even the pagan nations with whom Jerusalem was allied were shocked at her excesses.

Stage five: Jerusalem, the divorced (16:35–43). Here in the parable we see that her lovers will turn against her and strip her, her grieving God will divorce her and expose her to be stoned, her beauty will be destroyed, and she will find herself an unwanted foundling again.

Stage six: Jerusalem, worse than her sister Sodom (16:44–52). Both Samaria (capital of the Old Northern Kingdom) and Sodom were destroyed because of their moral disrepute, but they appeared righteous by comparison. Jerusalem was worse than the worst, so God's judgment was inevitable. But, even though Jerusalem was quick to condemn her two sisters, she was blithely unaware of the evil within herself.

Stage seven: Jerusalem, the restored (16:53–63). God's final word is a word of grace. God's temporary covenant will become an everlasting marriage bond, unaffected by the contingencies of time. God's love will triumph over any legal technicalities and the renewed people will recognize God as the true source of their being.

Again Ezekiel has sounded the third prophetic theme that there is hope for tomorrow. When Pope John Paul II visited his native Poland in June 1983, and met with Lech Walesa, he gave the people new hope. Later the Pope spoke on television about the problems of his homeland while the humorless

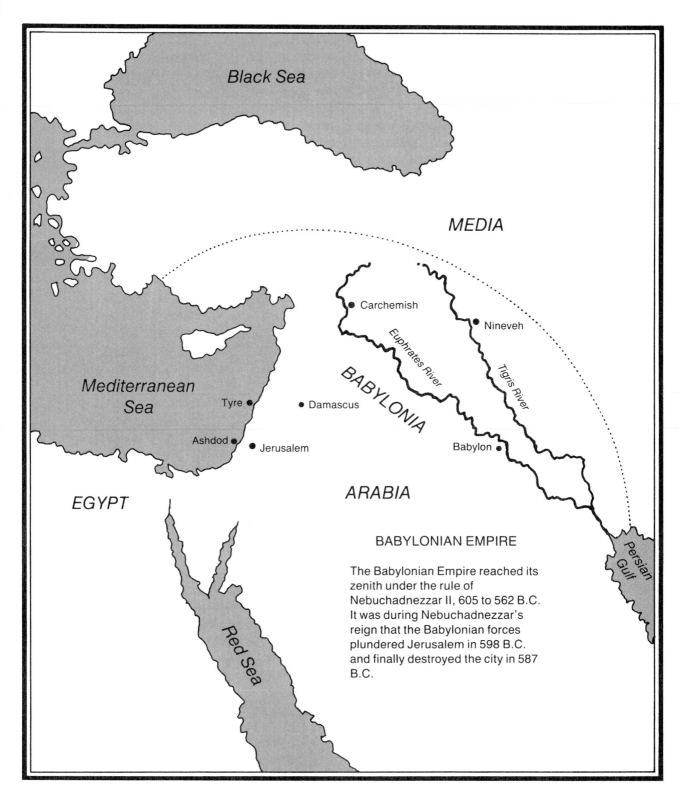

Black Sea

MEDIA

Carchemish

Nineveh

Euphrates River

Tigris River

Mediterranean
Sea

BABYLONIA

Tyre •

• Damascus

Ashdod •

• Jerusalem

Babylon •

EGYPT

ARABIA

Persian
Gulf

Red Sea

BABYLONIAN EMPIRE

The Babylonian Empire reached its
zenith under the rule of
Nebuchadnezzar II, 605 to 562 B.C.
It was during Nebuchadnezzar's
reign that the Babylonian forces
plundered Jerusalem in 598 B.C.
and finally destroyed the city in 587
B.C.

communist leader General Jaruzelski stood nervously by his side. A Warsaw professor watching the program said, "The general is actually trembling. Look at that. The whole trip is worth this moment." The Pope had given new hope to the Poles. We can't survive without the hope that God holds out to us, and this God does most generously.

The Parable of the Two Eagles

Just as Poland was sliced up by Germany and Russia at the beginning of the Second World War, so Judah was about to be carved up by Babylon and Egypt. Ezekiel's parable or political cartoon in this part of our lesson has to do with Judah's vascillation in foreign policy about 588 B.C. (17:1–24). Nebuchadnezzar, the "great eagle," had King Jehoiachin, the "young twig," in Babylon as a prisoner, and Jehoiachin was being cooperative. His uncle Zedekiah, the "seed of the land," had given his oath in the name of God to Nebuchadnezzar to be loyal, cooperative, and rule in his nephew's place. But Uncle Zedekiah had just switched his loyalty to Pharaoh Hophra (588–569 B.C.) of Egypt, the other "great eagle." By breaking his oath, Zedekiah had impugned the name and character of the God of Judah.

Ezekiel told the exiles that just as there was no hope in an alliance with Babylon, so there was no hope in an alliance with Egypt. Jerusalem's problems didn't arise in international politics, but in her own moral and spiritual decline. God's covenant forbad an alliance with Egypt (Deut. 17:16), so God simply could not bless an arrangement that contradicted the covenant. The lesson that God meant for them to learn was that the means must be in harmony with the ends; don't tell a lie for the greater glory of God, and don't murder in order to bring about moral conduct.

This is a lesson that every generation has to learn anew. The tragedy of Watergate for America was that people at the heart of our government were convinced that achievement was more important than character. Now we are having to learn all over again that character is crucial in every pew and pulpit. A top student was called into the president's office to account for an act of social disruption. The student snapped, "I'll bet there are not ten men on campus who wouldn't have done exactly what I did under the circumstances." Whereupon the president replied, "Has it occurred to you that you might have been one of the ten?" What is morally wrong can never be socially or politically right.

But the climax of the parable is a gracious one in that God promises to restore the chosen people to their land (17:24). Neither Babylon nor Egypt, neither Germany nor Russia, holds the key to history because God is in charge of His world.

Individual Responsibility: Neither the Good Nor the Bad is Transferable

Ezekiel's neighbors at Tel-Abib assumed that they were in exile through no fault of their own. They believed they were guiltless and suffering for the sins of former generations. It's all too human to blame someone else, but in shifting the blame to their ancestors it made the exiles lethargic and pessimistic about finding a current cure for their problems (18:1–32). They endlessly quoted a popular proverb which Ezekiel heard so often he grew tired of it, "The fathers have eaten sour grapes, and the children's teeth are set on edge" (18:2). Ezekiel finally fired back at them with the thought that God judges with discretion, "the soul that sinneth, it shall die" (18:4). The prophet claimed that God was always ready to punish evil and reward righteousness, and nothing had changed.

It is so characteristic of Ezekiel to promise hope just as he has pronounced doom. No one in exile was condemned for what others had done, and if only they would recognize their own responsibility for their prison, God would see to it that they got to go home. Responsibility meant guilt, guilt meant repentance, repentance meant forgiveness, and forgiveness meant a ticket back to Jerusalem. Only the responsible can be free. At the heart of the Good News is a forgiving and liberating Heavenly Father.

Lament Over a Family's Drive to Self-Destruction

Ezekiel next used a poetic lament—a kind of funeral dirge—to drive home the point to the exiles that we are responsible for creating our own trail of tears (19:1–14). He reviewed for them the last ten years of Jerusalem's tragic history. Judah, the lioness, had produced two cubs, Jehoahaz and Jehoiachin. Each reigned only three months and had produced very little. The first young man was exiled to Egypt and the second to Babylon.

Judah, now pictured as a vine, had recently produced a third king, Zedekiah—a strong branch—but he was just as bent on self-destruction as his two young predecessors. He, too, would soon end up in Babylon as a prisoner. So the exiles were not to think that their problems started outside themselves long ago and far away. The exiles needed to repent of their own contributions to their captivity, and only then would they find that their God was the great Liberator.

In my freshman year at college I took a history course, and on my first test I made a grade of nineteen out of a possible score of one hundred. It would have been great to blame anything but my own lack of study, but after sober reflection I finally accepted the distasteful idea that I got what I deserved. That shouldering of responsibility brought about a new resolution to study, a zest for the subject matter, and a determination to make a good grade in the course (which, fortunately, I did).

Father, I appreciate knowing You as my Liberator. You have freed me from my fears, freed me from my need to be perfect, freed me to trust You. AMEN.

WHAT THIS SCRIPTURE MEANS TO ME
Ezekiel 1—24

Our son, Brian, will soon be four years old. For the most part, he is an easygoing, fun-loving little boy. He loves books, music, and whatever cars, trucks, and buses he can get his hands on. My husband and I are constantly amazed and entertained by the things Brian learns, says, and does each day.

As one might expect, however, Brian is not a perfect little angel who never steps out of line or misbehaves. He is a normal child who occasionally tests his limits, gets into mischief, and tries to exercise his growing independence.

In the past few weeks, Brian has developed a rather annoying habit which I am hoping will be short-lived. Whenever I tell him "No," or try to correct his behavior, he responds by saying, "But, Mama . . ." followed by a contradiction of whatever I have just said.

Sometimes I feel like screaming when I hear those familiar words. Often I wish Brian would simply accept what I say without giving me an explanation. On occasion, I have staged a silent debate with myself: "Should I discipline Brian and risk hearing, 'But Mama . . .', or should I ignore what he's doing and avoid a confrontation?"

In most instances, it would be easier for me to avoid any conflict or disagreement. But, I realize that this temporary peace would have costly consequences later. Brian must learn gradually how to accept discipline and to respect the authority of parents, teachers, and other adults. He needs to learn good manners and proper etiquette. He needs to learn how to follow established rules and regulations. If I were to shirk my parental responsibility now, just to avoid hearing, "But, Mama . . ." and causing an argument, I would have to accept the blame of Brian's misbehavior and lack of discipline in the future.

In the second chapter of Ezekiel, a priest is commissioned by God as a prophet. He is sent to speak God's word to the people of Israel, who are impudent and stubborn, a nation of rebels (2:3,4). Later, the Lord says to Ezekiel, "I have made thee a watchman unto the house of Israel: therefore hear the word at my mouth, and give them warning from me" (3:17).

As I read verses 18 through 21, I was shocked by the grave responsibility which Ezekiel was given. Although he knew that the wicked would probably disregard his message of impending catastrophe, he was required to warn them anyway. Ezekiel had to be faithful to his God-appointed task even though his prophecy would be ignored or challenged. He himself would be accountable if he failed to fulfill his mission.

In a sense, all parents and educators share a responsibility similar to Ezekiel's. We must continually try to guide, discipline, and occasionally confront our children and students. We cannot shirk these duties simply because our counsel is sometimes ignored.

There are times when I feel burdened and overloaded by my roles as wife, mother, teacher, care-giver, volunteer, and homemaker. There are times when the weight of responsibility seems overpowering. During these times, I need to remember that God's power is far greater than my daily tasks. His Spirit will "enter into me and set me upon my feet" (2:2).

No matter what duties, jobs, or ministries I have, God will provide the strength, skills, and wisdom needed to perform them. I need only to seek Him, trust Him, and obey Him . . . one step at a time.

LESSON 2
Ezekiel 20:1– 32:32

The Fall of Jerusalem and Her Neighbors

Father, Forgive me for the many times I've slipped into chronic disobedience and indifference. Help me to repent; show me how to live in a way that honors You. AMEN.

Prophecies Against Judah Before Her Fall (20:1–24:27)

In Chapters 20 through 24 Ezekiel reviewed Judah's entire life for his exile audience and brought every element in society into focus for condemnation by God. Even as this review was going on, Nebuchadnezzar moved in on Jerusalem for the final kill in 588–7 B.C.

A Review of Judah's Horrible History

On August 14, 591 B.C., after seven years in exile, some of the exile leaders came to Ezekiel "to inquire of the Lord." He wouldn't talk to them about their questions, but instead the prophet gave them a history lesson to "cause them to know the abominations of their fathers" (20:1–44). For him their whole history was a story of breaking the covenant and chronic disobedience. The "elders" probably remembered only the glorious side of their tradition, but he showed them the darker, truer picture.

In response Ezekiel told the elders that the people of Israel had turned away from the faith in Egypt (20:5–8) when they had refused to turn from idols.

They had also turned away from God in the wilderness (20:9–26), where God's chief concern was to reveal Himself through His chosen people as a God concerned about all nations. Then when they got to Canaan, he reminded them that they had turned away from God by conforming to the pagan fertility cults and had thereby lost their usefulness to God (20:27–31). Once in the promised land, things got worse. They even misunderstood God's command about consecrating their children (Exod. 22:29) and turned it into bloody child sacrifices. In their twisted, warped thinking they turned the land of "milk and honey" into a kind of hell on earth, and they became so blind that they could justify anything by quoting God's words given to Moses at Mount Sinai.

Having made His case, God was now ready to pass judgment (20:32–44). The chosen people had to be purged before they could return to their homeland. Idolators couldn't go home, but the faithful remnant could, and when they got there, the Temple could be restored.

It's hard for us moderns to see how idols might have any bearing on us today. But the whole point of idol worship was to control God or the gods, to get a grip on one's own destiny, and to manipulate circumstances to one's own advantage. In other words, idolatry was a selfish extension of the self onto the outer world because the idolator didn't have enough confidence in God's care for his or her needs. Whatever a person depends upon—unless it's God—becomes an idol. And this object of dependence can be *anything*—art, wisdom, strength, money, honor, power, or a religion that will run errands for us. Idolatry today is believing in God after a fashion, but always in our own fashion. As Christians, whenever we believe that God is advantageous to ourselves, we are idolators.

We come now to a long, forceful proclamation of doom on Judah and Jerusalem in parable form, using the allegory of the sword, one of the conventional instruments of God's judgment (20:45–21:32). In the first scene (20:45–49) Ezekiel saw a thirsty forest fire consume the Negev, the desert south of Hebron.

Judgment by the Three Swords

Since his listeners didn't understand his meaning—a forest fire in a desert was too bizarre to imagine—he had to tell them more plainly that God had unsheathed His sword against Jerusalem (21:1–7). As a further object lesson God told him to sigh "with bitterness" as he made the prophecy to show the exiles how bitterly helpless Jerusalem would feel under siege. The prophet's public grief was not theater, because he really was heartbroken over the impending judgment of the Judeans. There is an emotional price to pay both by God and His minister when judgment has to be declared. The evangelist D. L. Moody said that when we preach on hell we should at least do it with tears in our eyes.

To make the judgment by sword even more dramatic, the prophet was told by God to do a sensational sword dance in front of his listeners (21:8–17). We have already seen how dramatic Ezekiel could be, and now he danced in an ecstatic state with flashing sword and warlike words to illustrate the destruction that would strike Jerusalem. The impact was as forceful as a minister today entering the pulpit and then storming the choir loft with an assault rifle. Ezekiel made his point—God, the swordsman *for* Israel (Exod. 15:3; Psa. 24:8), had now turned His sword *against* Israel.

The second sword mentioned in the parable was that of the Babylonian ruler, Nebuchadnezzar (21:18–27), and here prediction begins to blend into fulfillment. In 589 B.C. Judah and Ammon had signed a treaty of alliance to stubbornly resist the Babylonians, and Nebuchadnezzar was already on the march from the north to destroy them. The exiles must have taken heart when they heard about the treaty, but Ezekiel had to tell them that the alliance was a false hope. At the crossroads that led to Jerusalem or Ammon, Nebuchadnezzar had already decided to attack Jerusalem first. The city's capture was sure, for the pagan king was an instrument of judgment in God's hands.

The third sword was drawn against the Ammonites (21:28–32). The Babylonians had bypassed Ammon to get to Jerusalem, but that was only temporary. Ammon's evil and Judah's evil were alike,

The holocaust unleashed by Nebuchadnezzar's army on the city of Jerusalem in 587 B.C. reduced the city to ruins and the walls to a mass of rubble. Pictured here are two views of excavations at Jerusalem. The ruins in these excavation pictures date back to Old Testament times.

and their day of reckoning was not far off. All people have to live by the same moral standards or bear the consequences of their actions.

All Classes of People in Jerusalem are Guilty

God called the once holy city "the bloody city" and gave a long catalogue of its crimes (22:1–31). Social oppression and religious idolatry had brought about its ruin. Loss of faith in God by the people of Jerusalem had ushered in a moral decline. It was a "cut flower" city; cut from its roots like a rose stem, its bud would finally wither and die. The Old Testament prophets emphasized again and again that good conduct flows from a healthy faith. If God is absent, then might makes right, but righteousness alone was the source of Jerusalem's strength.

Through the prophet God made it clear that the "princes of Israel," its leaders, had set such an unrighteous example that no one could be surprised that the social fabric was rotten (22:6–16). They had caused God's person and purpose to be misunderstood, so He planned to send them into exile as well. Jerusalem had become a city of metal scrap, melted by the heat of God's wrath, and the dross was being gathered for elimination (22:17–22).

Then Ezekiel goes a step further as he insists that every responsible social group had become irresponsible (22:23–31). Consequently, there was no longer any reason for the city's existence. When a nation ignores its mandate from God, doom is its next and only step. All of us, Christians included, bear some responsibility for the ills of our society.

When Adolph Hitler rose to power in Germany in the 1930s, he set a high priority on controlling the church. Many German Christians moved easily from pride and patriotism to believing that God had a special place for the German people. For them it was a short jump to claim that Hitler's rescue of Germany from economic ruin was an act of God, demanding Christian assent. When Hitler made the Jews suffer, many of the people went along with his policy.

When the German Christians finally began to resist Hitler, it was too late. Any of us can be tempted to support an immoral agenda, or at least be neutralized in its opposition. But we can learn from the German Christians' experience that when we stay out of politics we can become supporters of evil. In the years before the war, Dietrich Bonhoeffer frequently quoted Proverbs 31:8 to the German Christians, "Open thy mouth for the dumb in the cause of all such as are appointed to destruction." Sadly, few of his fellow believers responded.

A Tale of Two Cities

Ezekiel told this story of two vulgar sisters to get his exile listeners to comprehend by shock God's attitude towards Judah's international political relationships (23:1–49). God is pictured here as the husband of Judah; Judah's lovers are her foreign alliances, which had religious as well as political implications. Ezekiel viewed foreign alliances as disloyalty to God because of their inherent dangers of syncretism and apostasy (2 Kings 16:7–19).

In the story told by the prophet, God took two prostitute sisters in Egypt and made them His wives (23:1–21). The first sister, Oholah—Samaria, or the ten northern tribes of Israel—continued to take lovers and was destroyed by the Assyrians in 722 B.C. Oholibah—Jerusalem, or the two southern tribes of Judah—turned out to be far more degraded than her sister, and was willing to bend to the strongest wind of political power, which at the moment was Babylon. Judah's political alliances led to the tragedy of moral deterioration and religious decay.

Just as the first lewd sister had been destroyed by the Assyrians, the second lewd sister would fall to her former nighttime lover—the Babylonians. Both sisters had failed in being faithful to God and His ten commandments, and now both had failed in life. Madness was the end result for both of them. Now, the exiles would have to relearn faithfulness to God if they had any hope of being restored to Jerusalem.

The Beginning of the End for Jerusalem

On January 15, 588 B.C., God told Ezekiel to mark his calendar, for on that day Nebuchadnezzar had begun his siege of Jerusalem (24:1–27). The prophet was then to announce the terrible day of attack to the exiles in far-off Babylon in the form of an allegory in which Jerusalem was a rusty pot and its people were flesh seething over a hot fire (24:1–14). Finally the pot was empty but left on the fire to burn itself clean. But the rust—the idolatry—had become so much a part of the pot that the flames could not burn it off. The lesson was clear. Idolatry had become so ingrained in Jerusalem that not even God could redeem it. Jerusalem had failed to be useful, and uselessness invites disaster. About eighteen months later, in the summer of 587 B.C., Jerusalem finally fell under the assault of the Babylonian army.

God's next instructions to Ezekiel must have been terribly shocking. God told him that his beloved wife was going to die (24:15–27). But he was instructed to forego the customary rites of mourning as a means of emphasizing his spiritual mission. When the people asked why he didn't mourn, he explained that his lack of grief was no more unusual than what would happen to them when Jerusalem fell. He was too numb for grief, and so would they be when the beautiful Temple in Jerusalem "died"—was demolished. Just as he controlled his emotions, so must they when they lost the central symbol of their faith. He was speechless now, and they would be speechless later. When the final news of Jerusalem's fall reached the exiles in Babylon by messenger, Ezekiel would once again have words of hope and restoration for them.

The God of All Nations: Prophecies Against Foreign States (25:1–32)

The underlying theme in Ezekiel's colorful writing is that God is an international God who, by His very nature, relates Himself to everybody everywhere. He cannot be identified with Palestine alone because He can leave Jerusalem anytime He wishes. Furthermore, all nations are morally and spiritually responsible to God, and no evil nation can escape God's punishment. Ezekiel drives home this point by saying that God's judgment is about to fall on seven of Judah's neighbors—Ammon, Moab, Edom, Philistia, Tyre, Sidon, and Egypt.

In the last section we saw that Ezekiel's wife had just died, and that he had started a period of silence, waiting for news to be brought that Jerusalem's Temple had been destroyed before he began to speak again. In Chapter 33 when he finally gets the news of Jerusalem's collapse, he begins to speak again as he gets a new sense of direction for his ministry. Chapters 25–32 fill in this gap of silence with his writings about God's word against foreign nations. Many of these oracles are in the form of poetry and not only show the prophet's gift for language but his remarkable insight into international affairs. Let's take a close look now at these words from his period of silence.

Ezekiel first directs his attention to Judah's close neighbors (25:1–17). The Ammonites were the descendants of drunken and incestuous Lot, Abraham's nephew (Gen 19:30–38). They were a sadistic group who showed malicious delight over Judah's fall (25:1–7). They were happy, not because God was vindicated, but because they were bestial, without compassion, heartless, and blind. And because the Ammonites laughed at the grief of others and seized their territory, they would be brought to grief. By Ammon's fall, God would be shown to be the Judge of all nations and the Author and Finisher of history.

The application of this is clear and immediate both to my own life and the life of my country. In the last few years several well-known Christian evangelists have lost their ministries through alleged misconduct. I am not to take delight in their disasters, but to feel personal grief for them and sorrow that the cause of Christ has taken a public smearing. And if I have any sense at all, I will let their troubles be an example to me of how not to allow greed or other vices to dominate my life. One of my teaching colleagues told me of a student that he called into his office for cheating on a final exam. I asked, "What did you say to her?" He replied, "I didn't say anything. I sat there and wept for her and with her." At the end of the Second World War, the United States rejoiced for a short time over the Allies' victory, and then set to work to rebuild the countries of its recent enemies, Germany and Japan. God is sovereign over all nations, and not just a chosen few.

Moab's sin (25:8–11) was insensitivity to the special mission that God had for Judah. They were delighted, as they claimed, that Judah's God was just

Oracles Against Ammon, Moab, Edom and Philistia

like any other god and could not or would not protect Judah. They could not see that God would judge them for the same sins that He had judged Judah. Edom (25:12–14) vengefully attacked the people of Judah when they were helpless, but God had not ordered the attack. Since Edom had assumed the right to practice the wrath of God, it would as a nation quickly learn what the wrath of God was really like. And because Philistia (25:15–17) had taken vengeful advantage of Judah, destruction now cast a dark shadow over her future.

The Fearful Future of Tyre (26:1–28:23)
Destruction Predicted

Tyre, situated on the Mediterranean coast one hundred miles northwest of Jerusalem, had been the seat of Phoenician commercial power since David and Solomon's day. The city was almost impregnable from land attack because it was built on an island connected to the mainland only by a causeway. Ezekiel clearly predicted its siege and destruction by Nebuchadnezzar (26:1–21). As soon as Jerusalem fell, the Babylonian king laid siege to Tyre. But after thirteen years of siege (585–573 B.C.) the city still stood. Nebuchadnezzar, in frustration, pulled his army away and gave favorable peace terms to Tyre. Ezekiel later admitted that his prediction was not fulfilled (29:18–20). Tyre finally fell to Alexander the Great in 332 B.C.

Tyre was condemned because it was a predator like Ammon and Moab. Tyre is pictured as gloating over the economic gain that would be hers when Judah and Jerusalem were completely conquered. The people of Tyre were eaten up with commercial avarice. The enmity of foreign nations would eventually destroy Tyre, and the rock island city would become just a bare rock where fishermen dried their nets.

Everyone assumed Tyre would last forever; it had stood for centuries as a symbol of permanence, but it would eventually become a symbol of the temporality of everything created by man. God had brought life out of the "deep" of chaos in creation (Gen. 1), and now God was assigning Tyre to return to Sheol or the Pit—a shadowy state of lifelessness, according to ancient thinking. Tyre would be wiped out completely. Only God can offer us permanence, a place of eternal life in His more immediate presence.

Recently, I conducted the funeral of a dear friend that I have known for half my life. We buried her body in a casket in the ground, but because she was a true child of our Heavenly Father I can say three things about her. I know where she is—in the more immediate presence of God clothed in a spiritual body or form that best expresses what she has become under God's leadership (1 Cor. 15). I know where she is placed in the Lord's presence—in a place that is best fitted for her Christian character, disposition, talents, and will. And I know what she is doing—she is actively growing in grace and knowledge, assuming larger areas of responsibility and infinitely expanding the love for others that she so ably demonstrated when she was with us. That's the kind of permanence I want for myself.

Pride and Shipwreck

Tyre is compared in our lesson to a perfectly beautiful ship constructed of the best wood by her builders. But she is wrecked in a storm and sinks to the bottom of the deep with all hands and cargo. Terror and mourning take place on the shore for the lost ship. The once great city was now a wreck (27:1–36).

How did Tyre move from excellence to disaster, because greatness doesn't necessarily lead to ruin. In Chapter 26 we saw that Tyre's fame led to pride, and it was this internal rot that brought the "good ship Tyre" to the bottom. Ezekiel draws a direct line between arrogance and shipwreck. Tyre was exceedingly competent but lacking in faith. Life brings disasters that no amount of competence can swim through without the help of God. Charles H. Spurgeon, the noted nineteenth-century preacher, said that we shouldn't be proud of race, face, place, or grace. The shipwreck of less competent people is certainly no reason to be smug about our own competence.

Vanity, egocentricity, arrogance, self-adoration, selfishness, and self-love are really synonyms for pride. The church has always recognized that pride, the overestimation of one's own self, is the basic sin against God. Pride is usually thought of as having four forms: pride of power—"I can make you do what I want you to do"; intellectual pride—"The way I see it is the best and only way to see it"; moral pride—"My conscience should be your guide"; and spiritual pride—"I speak for God, because I am closer to Him than you are."

The Pride of the Prince of Tyre

Ithobaal II, the ruler of Tyre, had committed the horrible blasphemy common to every dictator, of equating himself with God in wisdom and power (28:1–10). His very real successes in trading had caused him to believe that he was divine. Bertrand Russell said that every person would like to be God if possible, and some few find it difficult to admit the impossibility. The old Jewish proverb, "If you harden your heart with pride, you soften your brain with it, too," fits Ithobaal very well.

Ezekiel's criticism of him was that the king's achievements had obscured for him the truth that he was a mortal. He too soon forgot that God was the giver of the talents that had brought him to the pinnacle of success. But soon God would deliver him to the destroyers on history's stage, and then confine him to the Pit, to Sheol—darkness, death, the primeval chaos.

In verses 11–19 the king of Tyre is presented as innocent Adam in the Garden of Eden story at the creation (Gen. 2–3). But, as in the original story, the king of Tyre took the forbidden fruit: his city's growth in trade led him down the path of injustice and violence, and like the first Adam, he ended up outside the Garden in a broken relationship with God.

Ezekiel shows us how to interpret the Adam story, how to look at the prince of Tyre, and how to examine ourselves. Adam is the story of every person, not just an account of primeval origins. Adam is pictured in the Book of Genesis as an individual, as a collective—all people—and as a representative of humanity—he represents what I have done in my relations with God. Adam distrusted God, trusted himself instead, usurped the prerogatives of God, and ended up in a broken relationship with God and hostile toward Eve. The prince of Tyre's trade led to profit, profit led to greed, greed led to violence in the pursuit of more profit, and his wisdom was so perverted that he started calling himself "God."

In our own peculiar and perverse way we have repeated the Adam story in our lives with the same tragic results. But there is a major difference. We know that Jesus Christ, the "second Adam," can transform the original Genesis story and restore everything the "first Adam" lost (1 Cor. 15:42–50). We have the assurance of a return to an unbroken relationship with God and a reentry into the bliss of Eden.

In verses 20–23 Ezekiel says that the city of Sidon will receive the same judgment as Tyre. Sidon was just twenty-five miles north of Tyre and was probably guilty of the same catalog of sins. When Sidon, the last of Judah's arrogant neighbors, had been removed, the exiles would be able to return to the holy land without being harassed (28:25–26). The chosen people—the Hebrews—would once again dwell securely in their land.

The Decline and Fall of Egypt (29:1–32:32)

In these four chapters Ezekiel gives seven oracles against Egypt, Israel's neighbor to the south, with which there had been tense relations since the time of the Exodus. In her arrogant pride, Egypt had always been a false ally to Israel. Now God promised to bring His judgment—Egypt would still exist, but the country would no longer be a menace to other nations.

The First Oracle Against Egypt

This prophecy is dated in the winter months of 588–87 B.C. just before the fall of Jerusalem (29:1–16). If Tyre could be symbolized by a ship, Egypt could be symbolized by "the great dragon," the crocodile. Ezekiel pictured Egypt's judgment as the crocodile being dragged from the river and left to die on dry land, there to become food for birds and beasts. This harsh execution came about for two reasons: first, Egypt's false friendship to Judah, and second, her delusions of grandeur.

Egypt had forever been a vacillating, unreliable ally to Israel and Judah. Every time the Hebrews reached out to Egypt as a staff for strength—for support—it proved to be a brittle reed which broke when weight was put on it. Egypt's broken promises had proved disastrous in the past (Isa. 36:6; 2 Kings 18:21). Even while Jerusalem was under siege by Nebuchadnezzar, groundless hope for rescue by Egypt had been raised when the pharaoh's army made a diversionary military thrust from the south (Jer. 37). The old Jewish proverb, "A friend is one who warns you," certainly did not apply to Egypt.

The kind of friendship Egypt extended to Judah was one that took all but never gave anything in return. This selfish and false friendship undermined all human relationships, both personal and national, and invited judgment. At the beginning of the Second World War Hitler and Stalin signed a peace pact in order to divide up Poland, but the ink was hardly dry on the paper before Hitler's armies invaded Russia. True friendship will lay down its life for its friends (John 15:13), but a selfish friendship will withdraw at the slightest sign of cost. Fair weather friends are not friends at all. One of the wonderful things that Jesus said to us was, "I have called you friends."

Cecil Rhodes never participated in the gold rush days of Zimbabwe (then Rhodesia) to augment his fortune in diamonds. During the early leasing of the better gold fields, a friend of Rhodes lay desperately ill. The popular and wealthy Rhodes refused to leave the side of his sick friend and stayed by his bed, night and day, until he died. The Book of Proverbs holds up the ideal for us when it says, "A friend loveth at all times, and a brother is born for adversity" (Prov. 17:17).

Egypt invited disaster in the second place because of its ridiculous egotism. The people of Egypt were so self-centered that they deluded themselves into thinking they were self-made. They said, "My river [the Nile] is mine own, and I have made it for myself" (29:3). The powerful are unusually susceptible to believing that they are self-made. Over and over Ezekiel returns to the theme that pride goes before a fall. Prominence is just as much a gift of God as it is an achievement, and our boasting should be tempered by this realization. Because of Egypt's egotistical

In Chapters 29 through 32 Ezekiel gives seven oracles against Egypt, Israel's neighbor to the south. Relations had been tense between Israel and Egypt since the time of the Exodus. Now, according to Ezekiel, Egypt would be brought to judgment by God. Pictured here is a a scene synonymous with Egypt since ancient times. A view of the Great Sphinx of Gizeh with the pyramid of Khufu in the background. The sphinx symbolized the Pharaoh in his role as Ra, the sun god.

madness, God caused the land to be desolate from one end to the other for a full generation (29:10). Only as we empty ourselves of our egomania can we be filled with the presence of God. T. S. Eliot said that most of the trouble in the world is caused by people wanting to be important.

In the spring of 571 B.C., sixteen years after the first oracle, God promised to give Egypt to Nebuchadnezzar as a spoil of war, and fits into Ezekiel's growing hope that the exiles will eventually get to go home (29:17–21). The Babylonians had tried to capture

Second Oracle: Nebuchadnezzar's Prize

Tyre for thirteen years, but couldn't take the island fortress. The siege had been so expensive that Nebuchadnezzar needed some booty to pay for the campaign. So, in 568–67 his forces invaded Egypt, plundered it, and carried off its wealth. Egypt's pride had led to a very costly fall.

Third Oracle: Egypt's Humiliation

Under God's direction, history and nature would combine to strip Egypt of her egotism (30:1–19). The Babylonians would storm the country and God would dry up the Nile River. All of Egypt's splendor would topple. I've traveled in Egypt as a tourist and I've marveled at the country's extraordinary human achievments. I've also been sobered by the realization that no human structure can stand long without being subject to divine judgment. The proud and mighty are as vulnerable to God's powerfulness as are the weak and lowly. Humility and morality are the qualities that win in the long haul.

Sir Isaac Newton, probably the greatest scientific mind that ever lived, put it best when he said, "I do not know what I may appear to the world; but to myself I seem to have been only a boy playing on the seashore, and diverting myself now and then by finding a smoother pebble or a prettier shell than ordinary whilst the great ocean of truth lay all undiscovered before me." Humility is the garment that God Himself wears, and unless we learn to put it on we will not be humane to one another.

Fourth Oracle: The Fracture of Pharaoh's Arms

This prophecy was given in the spring of 587 B.C. Jerusalem was at the point of falling and the exiles in Babylon were hoping against hope that Egypt would come to their beloved city's rescue. In this symbolism of Pharaoh's broken arm—his military might—Ezekiel was telling the exiles that it was useless to hope for further help from Egypt (30:20–26).

God had broken Egypt's arm in order to leave her helpless when Babylon attacked. For the Judean exiles there was no hope of salvation from Egypt. In fact, to seek a military solution to what was basically a spiritual problem was foolish. National repentance was the necessary first step on Judah's road to recovery. Only the arm of God was strong enough to deliver them.

Ezekiel next describes the judgment of God upon Egypt with another figure, a cosmic tree. This oracle is dated in the summer of 587 B.C. when Jerusalem was finally being dismantled by her attackers. Addressed to the exiles in Babylon, the prophecy is about the Egyptian Pharaoh and his retinue. It is an allegory about a great tree that is cut down and falls into the Pit (31:1–18).

Pharaoh's greatness was like that of a great tree, superior to the cedars of Lebanon or the trees in the Garden of Eden, and envied by every tree in creation. But because of its haughty pride it would be cut down, shipped to Sheol, and there lie horizontally alongside other once great trees. No tree in the forest was safe if this great tree could fall.

In this allegory Ezekiel repeats several of the themes that we have already seen. An egotistical concentration on one's greatness coupled with a scorn of others leads to weakness in people and nations. True greatness is neither to be feared nor fawned over. Greatness is to be desired, but it can only be retained in humility and respect for others.

Then, too, when the great fall, the less than great get hurt. So many people are dependent upon the few great ones that when the tall tree falls it drags down a host of saplings. Two nights ago I was watching television news and saw a parachurch leader being tried in court for a major embezzlement scheme. To add to the sadness of the picture, several of his staff were being tried with him as lesser accomplices in the theft.

And Ezekiel again emphasizes the seventh theme of the prophets: The voice of authority is most likely not the voice of God. There were few voices in Ezekiel's day more authoritative than Pharaoh's, and few voices that were filled with more error.

Ezekiel gave this oracle in the early spring of 585 B.C., months after the exiles learned of the fall of Jerusalem. Here he returns to the image of Pharaoh as a crocodile, a river monster who flops about in the

Fifth Oracle: The Tall Cedar is Cut Down

Sixth Oracle: Pharaoh's Funeral

55

mud and fouls the water. God catches the dragon in a net and throws him on the land where animals and birds gorge themselves on his dead flesh (32:1–16).

The other nations mourned the death of the Pharaoh, but at the same time they were a little relieved that he was gone and no longer a danger to them. The troubled waters fouled by Pharaoh will run clear again once the troublemaker is banished. In the end God's judgment is always positive because he conquers the powers of evil and chaos. Egypt and Babylon may disturb the order of creation, but God is in the business of restoring peace and tranquility. Judgment subjugates evil, and only after that can God bring into being a better world.

Seventh Oracle: To Sheol With Egypt

The seventh oracle is dated somewhere in 586–85 B.C. and concerns the final resting place of Egypt in Sheol or the Pit, the land of darkness and shadowy existence (32:17–32). To the ancients this ghostly world was the grave of all humankind where the allegedly great lie without honor.

Ezekiel gives us a tour of the Pit and we see that all the nations of the past, both great and small, will be the grave companions of the Egyptians. This famous aggregation is guilty of crimes against humanity and Pharaoh is assigned a rightful place among them. They had made life so miserable for others that now life was denied to them.

The prophets of the Old Testament were the ones who began to hope for more than the Pit from a righteous God. This yearning found its fulfillment in the New Testament. In Christ we not only enjoy a fellowship with one another on this planet, but we enter a deeper and everlasting quality of life after the death of our physical bodies. We now turn in Ezekiel to the prophecies of hope and a taste of this life to come.

Savior, You know how I have sometimes created my own Sheol— by insisting on my own way; by neglecting my relationship with You. Thank You for reaching down and rescuing me each time. AMEN.

WHAT THIS SCRIPTURE MEANS TO ME
Ezekiel 25–32

As a child growing up in Detroit, Michigan, I thought our neighborhood was the grandest place on earth. Thirty-six children lived within two city blocks of our house. Every day after school, we gathered together for games of kick-ball, badminton, hide-and-seek, or jump rope. We took turns playing at each other's houses in small wading pools or on swing sets. We went exploring at Oshay Park, and fished tadpoles out of the pond. We looked for discarded pop bottles in the lot next to the corner gas station, and cashed them in for candy and gum. We went trick-or-treating together on Halloween, and later dumped our treasures out to sort into piles of "keepers" or "traders." We squeezed into the back of my dad's red pick-up truck and sang songs while riding to the ice cream store on hot summer evenings. We planned little skits, parades, and amateur gymnastics programs to perform for our neighbors and parents, charging them outrageous prices for admission and beverages.

But it was not merely the friends I had or the ongoing activities which made this place so special. I remember our neighborhood as being exceptionally beautiful. The houses were small and modest, but everyone took great pride in the area. Shrubs and lawns were always neat and trimmed. Leaves were raked in the fall and burned at the curb with great ceremony. During the winter months, the oldest kids in the neighborhood organized a snow-shoveling business, always managing to keep the sidewalks and driveways passable after each snowstorm.

And then came spring. Tiny buds began forming on the branches of the towering elm trees. With each passing day, more and more green appeared as leaves grew and took shape. By the end of May, the arms of these stately trees arched high overhead across our street, blocking out the scorching heat of the summer sun. Walking down Woodmont Avenue was like walking through a green, shady, fresh-smelling tunnel. It was gorgeous. I always looked forward to seeing nature's beautiful canopy every year. As I grew older, this wonderful sight became one of my fondest memories.

Ten years after my family moved away from Detroit, I returned to my former neighborhood for a sentimental visit. As I approached Woodmont Avenue, I could feel the excitement building within me. Even though many of the once-familiar stores and businesses were no longer there, I greatly anticipated my first glimpse of the giant elm trees lining the street where I had played as a child. As I turned the corner where Harris's Market used to be, my face fell, my foot instantly hit the brake pedal, and I heard myself saying, "Oh, no!" The beautiful elm trees which I had remembered so lovingly were gone. The street was bare and unprotected. No green, leafy archway beckoned me to pass beneath its outstretched arms. No towering trees with sturdy branches shaded me from the summer heat and sunlight. Our once attractive neighborhood now looked desolate, barren, and depressed. Dutch elm disease had robbed the entire area of its character and beauty.

In the first nine verses of Chapter 31, Ezekiel describes Egypt as a great cedar. Having experienced the beauty and subsequent devastation of the elm trees in Detroit, this image was a very powerful one for me. Egypt, like the great elm trees, had once been strong, powerful, and proud. "Its heart was proud of its height" (31:10, RSV). It towered above all the other trees (31:5) and was beautiful in its greatness (31:7). But Egypt's pride, vanity, and wickedness led to her downfall. This mighty nation was later broken and humbled. We are left with an image of utter desolation.

Sometimes I place too much emphasis on outward appearance. Too often, I concentrate on what people do—their occupations and activities—rather than on who they *are*. From now on I hope to always remember Ezekiel's image of the great cedar. Greatness is not determined by physical appearance, possessions, or positions of power and authority. These qualities can change in an instant. I pray that God will help me learn to focus on more lasting qualities which are far more important—character, attitudes, and values.

LESSON 3
Ezekiel 33–39

Prophecies of Hope: Return of the Exiles and the Defeat of Evil

---

Savior, Thank You for the hope I have in You—whether the road ahead looks promising or dreary, I know that You are my sure and lasting foundation. AMEN.

Our Scripture for Lesson 3 is characterized by an emerging and growing hope that the Judean exiles in Babylon will return to their home in Jerusalem. Ezekiel pictured a world restored to normal, and in a vision he saw a cosmic struggle in which evil rose up against God, but God finally defeated it.

Chapter 33 of the Book of Ezekiel serves to unite Chapters 1–24 with Chapters 34–39, giving a basis for a future hope and restoration to the Judean exiles. The watchman motif is repeated (see 3:16–21) and the problem of individual responsibility is again taken up (see Chap. 18).

A Review of Previous Oracles (33:1–33)

In Chapter 24, we saw that when Ezekiel's wife died he was commanded by God not to prophesy again until he heard the news of Jerusalem's collapse. When Ezekiel finally received news that Jerusalem had fallen, he publicly told his people the parable about the watchman (33:1–9). This marked the

The Renewal of Ezekiel's Vocation

renewal of Ezekiel's vocation and showed that his ministry was now headed in a new and more hopeful direction.

In Chapter 3 Ezekiel had been commissioned by God to be a watchman over the people of Judah. Now he expanded this commission into a full-blown parable to show the new direction that his ministry was going to take. The fall of Jerusalem was the beginning of a new and optimistic emphasis in his ministry as a prophet. Previously, Ezekiel had been a watchman, but he had not declared this publicly to the exiles. His vocation up to this point had looked to the past, but now it turned toward a future emphasis. Actually, Ezekiel's is one of the most optimistic voices in the Old Testament.

A prophet's task was to warn people of impending judgment. Then, if and when disaster struck, the people were fully warned. However, if the prophet failed to warn the people of the coming judgment, then the prophet would bear the responsibility and guilt. This was the kind of ministry to which Ezekiel had been called. His responsibility was to watch and warn the people, and when he had done that, his work was finished. The responsibility of the Judean exiles was to listen and react appropriately to God's word of warning.

With this new direction for his ministry Ezekiel must have been weighed down with his heavy responsibility. He could have agreed with President Calvin Coolidge, "One of the first lessons that a president has to learn is that every word he says weighs a ton." From now on it was up to Ezekiel to speak the words that would give encouragement to the exiles, and every word would "weigh a ton."

The interpretation of the prophet's parable is presented in two parts. In verses 7–9, Ezekiel was to alert his people to the evil that was about to strike them. The people's task was to heed Ezekiel's warning and turn to God.

Individual Responsibility and Corporate Guilt

The second part of the interpretation of the watchman parable is in verses 10–20. This is essentially a repetition of Chapter 18. The problem of individual responsibility naturally arose among the exiles when their corporate life fell apart. Ezekiel in his preaching emphasized both personal responsibility and corporate guilt. He stressed the fact that God did not wish the death of any person or any group. The prophet's instructions from the Lord were clear, "Say unto them, As I live, saith the Lord God, I have no pleasure in the death of the wicked; but that the wicked turn from his way and live: turn ye, turn ye from your evil ways" (33:11). The people, however, believed that the sins of their ancestors weighed so heavily on them that they had no chance of escaping disaster. But Ezekiel insists this was not the case. He made the point that no past evil or evildoer is beyond the hope and mercy of God.

The Hebrews continue to wrestle with the problem of evil and God's justice. In the balance was the idea that a person could lead a sinful life but be saved by a last moment repentance. Similarly, though, a person might after a lifetime of good living have all that cancelled by some last minute sinful act. Ezekiel now offsets this apparent dilemma by insisting that nobody is totally good, and a life of faith cannot be reduced to a credit and balance sheet of good and bad deeds. The people had made the mistake of applying a rigid idea of justice to the mercy and love of God. And since nobody was totally good, then everyone is saved by the grace of God. It was important for the people to understand that God's justice was forever tempered by mercy and the mystery of forgiveness. The only way that any of the Judean exiles could have a personal communion with God was through His mercy and forgiveness—justice was not God's last and final word.

Now, it was Ezekiel's task to declare the Lord's message to the people, and when he had done that, he had discharged his responsibility irrespective as to whether or not they accepted it. His ministry of warning was a service to the people. But the prophet's ministry was not only a privilege, it was also risky—he might fail and be rejected by his countrymen. Success was not a sure thing.

We next read, "And it came to pass in the twelfth year of our captivity, in the tenth month, in the fifth

The Fall of Jerusalem

61

day of the month, that one that had escaped out of Jerusalem came unto me, saying, The city is smitten" (33:21). Sometime during the winter of 587–86 B.C. an escapee from Jerusalem arrived in Babylonia with the news that the city had been taken by Nebuchadnezzar (33:21–33).

With the arrival of this news, as stated earlier, Ezekiel was released from the silence imposed upon him at the time of his wife's death. Also, as stated earlier, from this moment on the prophet became a preacher of hope rather than despair. At the same time, back in Jerusalem the prophet Jeremiah was carrying on the same kind of ministry with the people who were left there. Incidently, Jeremiah was to live only five more years after the destruction of the city. According to Jewish legend he was forcibly taken to Egypt by Judean refugees where he died a violent death.

Ezekiel's first message was to the survivors back in Jerusalem (33:23–29). It seems that the people who had survived Nebuchadnezzar's holocaust had failed to repent of their evil ways and turn back to God. Instead, they were consumed with the idea that since they were still in Judah, they and only they had claim to the land because it had originally been given to their ancestor Abraham. Instead of repenting of the sin that had caused Jerusalem's fall in the first place, they were trying to build their fortunes and then justified their actions in the name of religious conviction. They typified Pascal's belief that people commit evil most cheerfully when they do it in the name of religion.

The prophet now makes it clear to the people of Jerusalem why the city was destroyed. In blunt language he tells them that because they had failed to learn the lessons of history, God's judgment would strike the land of Judah and it would be turned into a dustbowl. Ezekiel reminds the people that it was their wicked pride that brought about their downfall. A close look at the prophet's words here reminds us of the theme, "pride leading to a fall." Pride and the lust for power blind us to the grace of God, but it is humility that keeps us steady and our values right. Legend tells us that Benjamin Franklin drew up a list of twelve virtues that he thought would help him attain moral perfection. In a conversation with an old Quaker friend he shared his list only to be told that he had omitted a most important virtue—humility.

Ezekiel then focused his attention on his fellow exiles (33:30–33). Among the exiles, Ezekiel had become a popular prophet because his predictions had been fulfilled with horrifying accuracy. He had become a center of great public interest, but his friends were not listening to his message. What he was saying didn't affect their understanding or

Ruins and partial restoration of the royal palace in Babylon. We have little hint today of the splendor of Babylon in the time of Ezekiel. Under Nebuchaznezzar the city covered an area of about two hundred square miles and was surrounded by a heavily fortified double wall on which were located two hundred and fifty towers placed at regular intervals. Eight gates provided access to the city.

influence their lives. They heard him talk of God's love but they didn't practice love.

Ezekiel had become a star performer among them, but his words could not penetrate their dull ears, and he was no more listened to in his popularity than he had been when he was unpopular. Consistent with human nature, they heard only what they wanted to hear. Only when Ezekiel's words were finally fulfilled would his ministry be vindicated. In spite of all his warnings, the Judean exiles had not understood that the calamities of history had been God's judgment. Hearing with their ears, they had not understood with their hearts. They could either learn or perish—they had no third choice.

A Future for the Exiles (34:1–37:28)
Wolves Among the Sheep: False Leaders

This next part of our Scripture lesson is united by the single magnetic hope that Israel would be restored to the promised land. Chapter 34 opens with a condemnation of the "shepherds" or the leaders of Israel, the kings of the land who had been set over the "flock" by God. The shepherd was a popular figure in the thought of the Hebrew people, and David himself had been a shepherd king. Frequently, the king was described as a shepherd of his people, and God was pictured in a similar manner on certain occasions (e.g., Psa. 80:1). In time the Messiah was described by the prophets as a Shepherd of God's people.

Ezekiel, continuing to talk about the fall of Jerusalem, focused his attention on the leaders and kings of the people of Judah and Israel. He condemned them as incompetent and delinquent shepherds (34:1–16). They were being judged for their past failures because the damage had already been done—as shepherds they now stood condemned by God. His indictment of these leaders was severe, since they had become little more than oriental despots, living in luxury and caring nothing for their subjects. Because Israel's leaders did not lift a finger to fulfill their pastoral duties, they had now ceased to be shepherds. While they had profited from their position of leadership, they had never assumed any responsibility. They had accepted the rights and privileges of a shepherd, but had ignored the responsibility.

Recently my daily newspaper carried an article with the blaring headline "Feds Investigating at Least 20 Preachers." The article states that the Internal Revenue Service and the Justice Department are poring over the financial books of twenty television and radio preachers. For more than two years the IRS has devoted about one hundred agents to investigate the finances of nearly three dozen television and radio ministries. To date the investigation has paid off with several convictions of theft, fraud, and graft. These individuals broadcasted programs in the name of Christ and solicited contributions on a national and international basis, only to take some of the money and feed their already lavish life-styles. The IRS might call it criminal, but Ezekiel called it dishonest greed and a dishonoring of their ministry.

Here Ezekiel again underscored the prophetic theme that much of the distress of the world is caused by false prophets. When their leaders fail, the innocent suffer. The Lebanese massacre of 1982 left this grim civilian toll: ten thousand dead, seventeen thousand wounded, and six hundred thousand homeless. We Christians still flinch when we remember John Wesley's words: "The world would be Christian were it not for the *Christians.*"

God: The Shepherd-Leader

Now comes the message to the people that God will be their Shepherd-Leader. In verse 15, we have God's unforgettable words, "I will feed my flock, and I will cause them to lie down." And God's complete ministry is described in these terms in verse 16, "I will seek that which was lost, and bring again that which was driven away, and will bind up that which was broken, and will strengthen that which was sick: but I will destroy the fat and the strong; I will feed them with judgment [I will shepherd them with justice]."

One of the oldest titles for God in the Old Testament is that of Shepherd (Gen. 49:24, Psa. 23). God will once again act directly as Israel's shepherd. Jesus said in John 10:11, "I am the good shepherd." He was picking up on this Old Testament theme to describe His own ministry. Whereas Israel's leaders enriched themselves at the expense of the flock—the people—

Jesus as the good Shepherd laid down His life for His sheep. As Shepherd, God's most fundamental concern was for His sheep. This gives us an insight into God's love for us. No shepherd can carry out his duties without sharing in the love of God for the individual sheep. Ezekiel's prophecies were now beginning to point in a positive direction.

The Future of the Sheep

This next part of our Scripture lesson tells us about the judgment of the sheep themselves (34:17–22), and at the same time it moves our attention forward to the future and the full restoration of the exiles (34:23–31). Continuing with the shepherd and sheep metaphor, we see that while the shepherd-leaders had been derelict, the sheep themselves bore some of the responsibility. Even among the sheep there were strong and weak ones—the good and the bad—and the stronger ones had exploited the weak for their own personal advantage. This shows us some of the perversity of human conduct even when we are supposed to be among equals. The strong sheep had destroyed the good things that they themselves could not use in order to keep them away from the weak ones. The strong sheep were completely unconcerned with the welfare of their weaker brothers. They were consumed by greed, and what they did not want they destroyed so that others could not have it.

We know from history that even in the most dire conditions the marginally stronger will seem to gain a little advantage over the weaker. From the concentration camps of the Second World War comes the testimony that even at the doors of death the weakest will be taken advantage of by their fellow inmates. It is even possible to use the gifts of God to shoulder a fellow believer aside. In the church at Corinth the Apostle Paul found some Christians using the gifts of the Holy Spirit to displace fellow saints in the worship service (1 Cor. 14:26–33).

But in the long run, the entire flock would be under the care of one shepherd, God's servant David (34:23). This reference is no doubt about the Messiah and His coming. The expression "my servant David" is not entirely clear, but it does point to the future where the covenant would be both renewed and reestablished. Just as David was a shepherd before he became king, so David's successor, the Messiah, would be a Shepherd-King and God's final good Shepherd. Ezekiel's words here were designed to bring an element of cheer to the exiles in Babylon. Once the bad kings had been banished and the Messiah was in place, the covenant relationship would be renewed on a permanent basis. We remember that the third theme common to all the Old Testament prophets was that the messianic vision offered hope for a better tomorrow.

Next, God promises His people a covenant of peace, which meant the absence of danger as well as security in a land of abundance (34:26–27). Then, blessings would come like showers, the yoke of slavery would be removed, and the exiles would no longer experience hunger or be outcasts. In this blessed state, they would know for certain they could depend on God. The whole substance of Chapter 34 is summed up in the closing verse, "And ye *my* flock, the flock of *my* pasture, are men, and *I am your God,* saith the Lord God" (34:31, italics mine). The covenant relationship between God and His people would be firmly reconstituted and the happy ending would be a transformed life and society.

Next comes the prophecy against Edom (35:1–15). Mount Seir is another name for the nation of Edom, those cousins of the Israelites who were the descendants of Jacob's brother Esau. Edom was located at the south end of the Dead Sea which is today a part of the territory of the kingdom of Jordan. Edom was destined for destruction because as a nation it had taken advantage of Judah in the time of that nation's calamity.

News had reached the exiles in Babylon of Edom's complicity in Judah's collapse. As soon as Judah fell, the Edomites began to seize the land for themselves. Edom had always hated the people of Judah and Israel, and now that hatred was mixed with envy. Ezekiel makes the same point as the other prophets: Any nation that harbors hate toward its neighbor will attract the same kind of hate. No people can

The Destruction of Cousin Edom

make themselves secure by violence. Every nation needs to learn the act of forgiveness in order to survive. Hate and greed combined make a dangerous mixture. The people of Edom had cast a boomerang of hate that would ultimately come back to destroy them.

The Middle East is still in turmoil today as little children are being taught an implacable hatred for the "enemy." Former Secretary of State Henry Kissinger has said that there are reasonable solutions to the problems in that part of the world, but there are not enough reasonable people there. Hatred, greed, and the lost art of forgiveness are laying the foundations of a Third World War. I have a dear friend whose Georgia family name was originally Sherman. But after the northern General Sherman burned Atlanta during the Civil War the family had to change its name to Sharman to avoid the hostility of their southern neighbors. The curse of hostility in Ezekiel's time all too accurately mirrors the cancer of bitterness and unforgiveness in our own day.

Otto von Bismark, Prussia's "Iron Chancellor," carried the bile of bitterness and resentment like a backpack. One morning he proudly announced, "I have spent the whole night hating." This inner seething finally broke his health. Hatred was his passion, and he died at the age of eighty-three, an embittered, cynical, desperately lonely man, miserable and self-consumed. We either destroy our hate by the grace of God, or it destroys us.

The Restoration of New Israel

The prophecies of doom against Edom in Chapter 35 are now balanced by prophecies of hope addressed to Israel in Chapter 36. Throughout his messages Ezekiel uses the larger term *Israel* to signify all of God's chosen people, and not just the citizens of the tribe of Judah. Edom had recently helped destroy Judah, but now its doom was sealed. And while Judah now was devastated, by the mercy of God it had a bright future. Since the surrounding nations had rejoiced in Jerusalem's destruction because this gave them an opportunity for pillaging booty, these nations would now suffer the same fate (36:1–7).

Nebuchadnezzar of Babylon had left Judah in

ruins, but it would rise and live again. The postwar chaos in Judah would soon disappear and Judah would be restored to its former prosperity and beauty. The message was clear. As soon as the exiles confessed their guilt, God would give them a bright future. God's word of judgment was not His final word, and the time of restoration was at hand. The darkness would be swept away and God's mercy and love would triumph.

The surrounding nations might be happy about Judah's dire predicament, but God would see to it that His name was vindicated. God's true character and person would emerge in the rebuilding of Judah (36:8–15). God's ultimate purpose in restoring His chosen people was to reveal Himself to all the people of the world. It is true that the pagan nations thought that God was too weak to keep His people alive. They didn't understand that God had allowed Judah's citizens to suffer to point out their sinfullness and their unrighteousness. But God would show Judah's neighbors that once His chosen people were cleansed and restored to their land, His name would be honored everywhere. This would be a fulfillment of the fifth prophetic theme—that the people of Israel were God's means or avenue for ushering in peace and justice.

A New Heart and Spirit

In the second part of his ministry Ezekiel hammered home to the exiles in Babylon the idea that God would resurrect them from the death of captivity and restore them to their promised land. As they looked around at their dismal situation, they must have thought Ezekiel was crazy, for it certainly didn't look as if God had a place for them in the future. But Ezekiel showed his confidence in the power of God by continually asserting that the Hebrew exiles would be raised from death to a new life. There was hope!

The prophet knew, though, that the people needed a change at the very center of their personality. And in speaking of this change Ezekiel gives us the essence of his theology (36:16–38). Outwardly, to Judah's neighbors, God's relationship with His chosen people was a failure and a disaster. From all practical appearances they were a failure and so was their God. In fact, we understand from the prophet's wording here that God was concerned and possibly embarrassed by the interpretation Judah's neighbors placed on all that had happened.

But Ezekiel saw that God's original purpose in selecting the people of Israel to be His chosen people would be fulfilled. Their old spirit of evil and disobedience would be replaced with a new spirit open to God's will and wishes. God would take the initiative in bringing about this character change among His people—a change that would cause their pagan neighbors to become aware of the true nature of God. And with this change would come new life for the Hebrew people.

Several years ago we were electrified by the story of Dr. Christiaan Barnard transplanting a new heart into the body of Phillip Blaiberg of Cape Town, South Africa. Following that successful operation, Dr. Barnard walked into Mr. Blaiberg's hospital room one day carrying a plastic box containing Blaiberg's old heart. The eminent surgeon said, "Do you realize that you are the first man in the history of mankind to be able to sit as you now are and look at his own dead heart?"

Phillip Blaiberg's next dramatic moment came when he met the woman who gave him new life by granting the surgeons permission to transplant the heart from her husband who had just died into the body of Blaiberg. In reflecting on that moment, Blaiberg said, "What do you say in such circumstances? She had lost a life; I had gained one."

God's promise as given by Ezekiel to the Judean exiles was even more electrifying: "A new heart also will I give you, and a new spirit will I put within you: and I will take away the stony heart out of your flesh, and I will give you an heart of flesh. And I will put my spirit within you, and cause you to walk in my statutes, and ye shall keep my judgments, and do them" (36:26–27). Jesus' words several centuries later convey this same truth to Christians in all of time, "I am come that they might have life, and that they might have it more abundantly" (John 10:10b).

God's new covenant with the restored Hebrew exiles would involve a radical inner transformation of their character, and it was through this dramatic change in their lives that God would reveal His true nature to all humankind. While Israel's future would no longer take the form of an independent nation state, the Hebrews would be recognized as God's chosen people who were determined to do His will.

The practical lesson in all of this for us is that our lives are to be avenues through which God's holiness and character can be made known to the entire world. It is a sobering thought to realize that the only God some people will ever know about is the One they see in us. It is also interesting to note that the new heart and spirit of the Hebrew exiles would be preceded by a symbolic sprinkling of fresh water (36:25). For the Christian, baptism serves as a similar symbol, for it is an outward manifestation of an inward change.

Only the person with a new heart and a new spirit can show the world that our Lord is a universal and mighty God who loves all people. Stephen in the Book of Acts (Acts 6–7) was one of the first of the early Christians to understand that the good news of Jesus Christ was for gentiles as well as Jews. He understood that God was not localized in Palestine and that the Temple in Jerusalem was only one of many places where He could be worshiped. Stephen understood that Christianity was a world religion open to all people in all time.

Pastor Martin Neimoller was a prisoner at Dachau concentration camp during the Second World War. From his cell he watched every day as prisoners went to their deaths on the gallows. He could hear their cries, curses, and prayers. The gallows became his teacher as he was haunted by this question, "When they hang me will my last words be, 'Father, forgive them' or will they be 'Criminals! Scum!'?" Niemoller said that if Jesus had cried out in vengeance from the cross, there would have been no New Testament, no church, and no Christian history. Long before Jesus proved it, Ezekiel was telling the Hebrew exiles that God was a forgiving, restoring God, and it takes a new heart, a new spirit, a "born again" experience for us to enter into God's attitude of loving and forgiving everyone.

The Valley of the Dry Bones

Two real life problems lie in the background of Chapter 37. First, Judah was like a dead nation without any future hope. Second, the tragic rupture that occurred in 922 B.C. between Judah in the south and Israel in the north had not been healed; there was still a great schism between them. Ezekiel deals with these two problems in this part of our Scripture lesson (37:1–14).

When the exiles received news that Jerusalem had fallen, they felt as though they were dead people with no future. They were like a valley full of dead men's bones. In a number of Ezekiel's visions, he may be reflecting a subconscious feeling growing out of some conscious experience. He probably had seen dead, dry bones on the battlefields. In this vision, he saw all of Judah and Jerusalem in a state of hopeless death. The exiles had no more hope of returning to Jerusalem on their own than of putting flesh on a skeleton and saying it was alive.

As Ezekiel looked out across "the valley which was full of bones," God asked him the question, "Can these bones live?" Ezekiel's normal response would have been, "Of course they can't live, anyone would know that." But instead he answered, "O Lord God, thou knowest." Then God told him to preach to this valley of dry bones, and the results were astonishing. The bones were restored to life, and before the prophet's startled eyes, the bodies got on their feet and returned to the promised land.

Ezekiel then reported this remarkable vision to his countrymen—the exiles. The message was clear. While the collapse of Jerusalem had seemed to be the end of the life of the chosen people, by the power of God they would be restored to their original homeland. This points to the capacity of God to raise the dead and to give new life. God has the power to impart fulness of life to all creatures. God promises to open the graves of all those who have died and make them live again. The exiles felt that they were living in a grave, but God promised them that He would put His spirit within them and they would live, and in their own land (37:14). Now we begin to see why Ezekiel is thought of as one of the most optimistic voices in the Old Testament.

Next, Ezekiel was commanded by God to take two sticks. Upon one he was to write the name Judah—the southern kingdom—and upon the other he was to write the name Joseph—Israel, or the northern kingdom. Then he was to join the two sticks together, and by this act to demonstrate that God intended to reunite the divided kingdom of David as He had promised (37:15–28). Ezekiel never accepted the separation of the north and the south, and throughout his prophecy he used the old name of Israel, rather than just Judah, when he talked about the covenant people.

The tragedy of the separation of the kingdoms of Israel and Judah had continued across the years with little hope for healing. But now God promised the Hebrew exiles that north and south would be their homeland when these two states were brought together once again under God's rule in His time. All the idols and evils that had led to the split in 922 B.C. would be removed, and the kingdom would be united under a "new David." In the midst of the united kingdom would be God's sanctuary representing His presence and purifying power. All of God's people were important to Him and only God could bring unity out of the former fracture. Simply put, God's salvation extended to all people everywhere and not just to a limited few.

Two years ago I took a night airplane flight from one city in the Orient to another. I was the only white westerner among the two hundred passengers, and not even the flight attendant spoke English. I ate their strange (to me) food and listened to their strange (to me) language, wrapped in my own cocoon of silence and incomprehension. While this wasn't the first such experience I'd had, my cultural isolation gave me the opportunity once again to reflect on the truth that God loved each one of the two hundred passengers just as much as He loved me. None of them could speak "Texan," but each one was a potential brother or sister in Christ.

Judah and Israel Reunited: A Story of Two Sticks

The Lord then made it clear through Ezekiel to the Hebrew exiles that only David's heir could rule over this new ideal state (37:24–25). Under his rule there would be perfect obedience and God's statutes would be obeyed. And an everlasting covenant of peace would be established among this restored and united people as God promised, "I will be their God, and they shall be my people. And the heathen shall know that I the Lord do sanctify Israel, when my sanctuary shall be in the midst of them for evermore" (37:27–28).

God's Final Defeat of Cosmic Evil (38:1–39:29)

In this part of our Scripture Lesson Ezekiel looks ahead to the time when God would win a cosmic victory over all the forces of evil in the world. At that time, too, a united Israel would be restored to the land of Palestine and would remain secure and peaceful in God's covenant.

Visions and Prophecies about Gog–the Essence of Evil

The series of prophecies about Gog in Chapters 38 and 39 are among the most difficult parts of the Book of Ezekiel to understand and interpret. Gog and the land of Magog should be understood in symbolic terms as the very epitome of evil in history. Attempts to identify these two figures with historical places or political powers have met with very little success.

I think Ezekiel is picturing darkness and light in a tense struggle on the stage of history. He pictures the battle reaching its climax when the final victory by God is won. This immense concept should not be lost because the format is expressed in such a concrete way. This figure is to be taken seriously but not literally. All the place names listed in this table of nations represent the ends of the earth as Ezekiel knew them. All evil would gather together with Gog from the land of Magog in the north and descend upon restored Israel and threaten its security. The characters of the drama are both of this earth and supernaturally above the earth.

In the New Testament (see Rev. 20:8) these chapters are interpreted in supernatural—apocalyptic—terms, and are seen to refer to a still distant future. Ezekiel may have been referring to the coming destruction of Babylon, but he could not openly say this for fear that the Hebrew exiles might be abused by the government. We must be careful not to interpret these prophecies by assuming that they're simple predictions of our own day. Though people and places in apocalyptic literature can frequently be identified, they should rarely be taken literally because they are part of the stage setting of the literary drama.

The final teaching of these chapters underscores the fact that God is the director of all human history and that evil wherever it is found will ultimately be subject to His judgment—God will demonstrate His holiness to people everywhere by overcoming evil

A restoration in Babylon of an area sometimes referred to as "Procession Way." Even with the partial restoration it is difficult to picture the grandeur of the ancient city as Ezekiel and Daniel knew it. Built on both sides of the Euphrates River, it has been said that approximately nine-tenths of the city area was devoted to gardens and parks.

once and for all. Ezekiel's vision is an allegory of the last days and points to God's conclusive triumph.

God's Positive Defeat of Evil

In Ezekiel's oracle now he sees that when the people of Israel are restored to their promised land they will be an easy target for their foreign enemies who were always attempting to better themselves economically by plundering God's people. But the prophet also sees that the eternal God of good and of order will move to confront these forces of chaos and evil (38:1–9).

To the foreign powers the returned exiles might appear defenseless and an easy mark, but God would be their defender, and Ezekiel saw that in the final cosmic battle the forces of righteousness would overcome the forces of evil. It is true, of course, that the battle between good and evil has been going on since the beginning of time, but here Ezekiel projects it onto a supernatural—apocalyptic—screen to illuminate his ultimate faith in God's victory. He sees that evil will be conquered by the direct intervention of God in human history—God's will *will* be done. And now, as then, the affairs of the world are not as bleak and dismal as they may appear on the surface because God will move people and events toward His ultimate purposes.

Gog's Greed versus God's Greatness

The prophet now paints a vivid picture, rich in the imagery of that time, of the battle between Gog—symbolic of Israel's enemies and the forces of evil—and God. He sees the combined enemies of God's people arrayed in awesome force against them. However, God musters all the forces of nature and of good against the attackers, and in that final cosmic battle God will be declared the winner (38:10–23).

This age-old war between the good and the bad, projected here by the prophet on an apocalyptic screen, gives us an extraordinary statement of faith. The people of Israel and Judah were captives and fugitives, and the other nations of the ancient Near East were locked in bitter struggles for supremacy. It was a world of chaos in which, for all practical purposes, the forces of evil had things going their way. But even in the midst of this gloomy scene Ezekiel had the confidence to say in symbolic language that God would prevail. Evil in its four forms of grisly ugliness, ignorance, suffering, and sin will be eradicated from the world scene. And this will be achieved so that people everywhere will recognize the greatness of Israel's God—the majestic Creator who is not aloof but who is intimately concerned with everything that touches humankind.

The Total Defeat of Evil: the War to End All Wars

As Ezekiel moves into his next oracle, he repeats the description of the total defeat of Gog (39:1–6). And he repeats, as well, the theme that Gog's downfall is for the purpose of illuminating God's greatness to the pagan nations of the world (39:7–8).

Next, in verses 9 through 20, Ezekiel paints a vivid picture of the defeat and destruction of Gog—the forces of evil in the world. Once again, the apocalyptic language used here is to be taken seriously but not literally. The prophet pictures this as a war to end all wars. In this ultimate and complete victory God's power will be recognized by all people everywhere. Now, the people of the world will see that the subjugation and exile of the people of Israel and Judah were not signs of God's weakness but demonstrations of His judgment of their sin. This would open the way for a new world in which there would be no evil and no war.

The Exiles Return Home

With the defeat of evil and with the recognition of God's power comes the assurance to the Hebrew exiles of their return home (39:21–29). But for it to become a reality, they had to accept it and believe it and persevere. They, and we, can take to heart the reactions of the Duke of Wellington when his British army achieved victory over the opposing French forces. He said, "British soldiers are not braver than French soldiers; they are only brave five minutes longer." The Hebrew exiles had to believe Ezekiel's good news of deliverance long enough for it to become a reality.

The writer of the Book of Hebrews defined the kind of faith God's people in every century are to have, "Now faith is the substance of things hoped for, the evidence of things not seen" (Heb. 11:1).

Then comes those marvelous words of assurance as through His prophet God tells the Hebrew exiles that in response to their perseverance and faith, "Neither will I hide my face any more from them [the people of Israel]: for I have poured out my spirit upon the house of Israel" (39:29).

Ezekiel didn't live long enough to see the fulfillment of God's promise. He had no idea when that would occur, but he was fully convinced that it would happen. Because of this, Ezekiel emerges as one of the most hopeful of all the Old Testament prophets. And like him, we Christians are to be a people of hope. The Apostle Paul in writing to the beleaguered Christians in Rome expressed it well when he said, "Now the God of hope fill you with all joy and peace in believing, *that ye may abound in hope,* through the power of the Holy Ghost" (Rom. 15:13, italics mine).

Ezekiel's message to the Hebrew exiles and to Christians of every century is that God is a forgiving and restoring Lord. His grace reaches out to us in all of the circumstances of life; we are never out of reach of His love and grace.

Lord, Fill me with the joy and peace that comes with believing—let me abound in Your hope, through the power of the Holy Ghost. AMEN.

WHAT THIS SCRIPTURE MEANS TO ME
Ezekiel 33—39

In August of 1988, our family spent two glorious, fun-filled weeks at Carolina Beach near Wilmington, North Carolina. We rented a modest little apartment located right on the ocean. Because the fall school term was approaching, most vacationers and tourists had already come and gone. As a result, we felt as if we had the entire beach to ourselves. The condominiums and apartment buildings around us were for the most part uninhabited. Our colorful beach umbrella stood alone in the sand. We enjoyed unimaginable peace, privacy, and solitude.

Many of our days at Carolina Beach were spent in a rather predictable fashion: early walks along the shore searching for unusual shells to add to our collection, riding the waves in the ocean, building sand castles close to the water's edge, playing with the Frisbee; munching on snacks while reading books and magazines which had been saved for this special time.

On several occasions we drove to Wrightsville Beach, fifteen miles away. For some reason, the water appeared clearer there, and especially beautiful next to the almost-white sand. There were many attractive yachts and sailboats to look at and admire. The town itself was quaint in its layout and structure, and the restaurants, businesses, houses, marina, and the beach itself seemed "picture-perfect."

Several days after we had arrived back home, we heard a disturbing report on the evening news broadcast. Several plastic bottles, syringes, and containers of medical waste had washed up on Wrightsville Beach. Vacationers had been cautioned against swimming in the immediate area.

This report absolutely sickened me. I couldn't believe that the white sand of Wrightsville Beach had been tarnished and invaded by carelessly discarded vials and plastic bags. My mind just couldn't comprehend it.

After a few moments of astonished silence, I slowly began to recall other reports which I had heard recently—similar kinds of waste had washed up on other beaches on the east coast. For some reason, those broadcasts hadn't had the same impact on me. I had heard about this environmental problem before, but I hadn't paid much attention to it.

Suddenly Ezekiel's words hit me full-force: "He heard the sound of the trumpet, and did not take warning" (33:5a RSV). Environmentalists have been sounding the trumpet for years—about growing problems with pollution, the diminishing ozone layer, garbage disposal, acid rain, and other situations which affect the health and safety of people throughout the world. We are not being good stewards of our precious environment. God's awesome creation is being devoured, disgraced, and destroyed.

My sincere prayer is that all people will listen to the warnings and take action. We need to improve our attitudes and change our life-styles. We can no longer ignore the sound of the trumpet.

In Chapter 36:8–15, Ezekiel proclaims God's promise to His people: Israel will be returned, restored, and released from disgrace. This is my hope and vision for the future of our planet. May we all learn from our mistakes and strive toward wholeness and rebirth.

LESSON 4
Ezekiel 40-48

Ideal Israel: The Symbolic Shape of the Temple and the City of God

Lord, Help me to see You in this lesson the way You want me to—in a way that makes greater demands on me, in a way that pulls me more out of myself and into You—that allows me to be more what You're calling me to be. AMEN.

In Chapters 40–48 we see the prophet-priest Ezekiel come to the last, greatest, and most controversial of his visions. Like a loving architect he sketched plans for the rebuilding of the Temple and then surveyed the territory of Jerusalem and each of the Twelve Tribes. He was so precise and exact in his details and measurements that as modern readers we get lost in all his "cubits." (A "cubit" was an ancient linear unit based on the length of the forearm, usually from seventeen to twenty-one inches. We would say, "About a foot and a half.") His plan is not too difficult to follow, however. It is the picture of a "perfect" Temple, so alone in its holiness that it can serve as God's throne from which He will rule Israel and the world.

We have already seen that even though Ezekiel preached the same seven themes as the other prophets, he is absolutely unique. He is new, though, in the great emphasis that he places upon individual responsibility. He is also more intense than the other prophets in his use of the prophetic method, so much so that many Bible students think of him as the creator of apocalyptic and allegory. Ezekiel was certainly the most ecstatic of the writing prophets. Again, in helping the Hebrew exiles to believe in and hope for a future, he painted a very specific picture of that future in the chapters that we are now going to study.

To put it simply, Ezekiel dismissed the idea of rebuilding the state of David—the monarchy—and concentrated upon the shaping of a theocracy where God would be recognized as the supreme civil ruler. This way, Israel would be ruled from the Temple by priests, and the community of the new covenant would be ecclesiastical—a church—rather than political. No other prophet had pictured the future in this way.

Ezekiel's priestly view had a deep influence upon the religion that came out of the exile period—Judaism. Since his became the actual pattern of Jewish life after the exile, he can be credited with establishing its general character and giving it shape. Because of this Ezekiel is often called the Father of Judaism.

Unfortunately, he never had the great worldwide missionary vision of the Isaiah writer in Chapters 40–60. He yearned as much as the other prophets did for God's universal kingdom, but he never saw a place for vicarious sacrifice—the innocent suffering for the guilty—or for the chosen people losing their lives in a superb missionary effort for the gentiles. Instead, Ezekiel saw restored Israel devoting her energies to guaranteeing her own purity and strength. In practice this turned into isolationism and provincialism and led eventually to the separatist movement known as Pharisaism. The distorted legalism of the Pharisees was the major human ingredient in the crucifixion of Jesus.

Ezekiel may not have had the universal vision of Isaiah, but he did shape the flowering of the postexilic religion into Judaism. Christianity in part owes its existence to Ezekiel. The church grew directly out of the concrete life and institutions of postexilic Judaism as well as the dreams of the prophets. Without

Ezekiel, Christianity would have had great difficulty coming into being. Actually, he gave us a picture of the church before the New Testament church existed.

You may need to be warned ahead of time that Ezekiel will overwhelm you with architectural details. But that is his literary way of getting us to see the larger picture. He starts on the inside and works out. On one occasion my journalism teacher in high school took our class to the state's leading and largest newspaper for a tour of the giant plant. During our visit of several hours we saw the "nuts and bolts" of how a newspaper was produced, and came away with awe at how large the operation really was. Ezekiel will do the same for us here about the restored Israel.

In the year 573 B.C. (40:1–2) the prophet had a vision about the restored Temple, which is among the last of his dated prophecies. It happened on the twenty-fifth anniversary of the destruction of Jerusalem and occurred during the latter years of his life. Central to any restoration of the city was the Temple, but without God's presence the Temple would be useless. In the prophet's vision he saw the Temple in exacting detail, and then met God Himself in it.

Ezekiel's prophecy opened with a grand vision (Chapters 1–3) and ends here with an equally grand one. He had seen God leave the Temple (Chapters 8–11), and then he saw Him return. Ezekiel saw Jerusalem and Judah collapse and die, and he then saw their resurrection and return to the promised land. After years of reflection he began to see what the ideal Israel of the future would be. Now began the vision of what the symbolic restored Israel would look like (40:1–4). As in Chapters 38–39, the writing is apocalyptic in style.

In this scene Ezekiel was transported once again to the Holy Land in a visionary visit (see Chapters 8 and 11) and set down on a high mountain overlooking the city, possibly the Mount of Olives. His heavenly guide, who was probably the same guide as the one in Chapters 8 and 9, was rebuilding this time rather

The Measurement of the Temple (40:1–42:20)

A New Vision

than destroying. Now Ezekiel was told to listen and watch carefully because what he was about to see was very important.

I know that these chapters are hard for a modern reader to follow because they give exacting attention to details and measurements for a building that existed only in the prophet's imagination. We don't seem to get much spiritual nourishment out of cubits and blueprints. And we don't come from a priestly background like Ezekiel's. Consequently, we have little interest in a building that will never be built. But if we will stick with the prophet and his guide on their tour, we may begin to grasp the eternal principle that the essence of our existence is to be found in the knowledge and worship of God. With St. Augustine we may come to say of the Lord, "Our hearts are restless until they rest in Thee." God is with us, and our lives are completed in our worship of Him.

The Outer Court of the Temple

As Ezekiel's angelic guide gave him a visionary tour, the prophet took note of everything and the measurements as they were called out by his guide. According to the typical Temple gate plan of that day, dating back to the tenth century B.C., his tour began at the East Gate of the outer wall. There was also a North Wall Gate and a South Wall Gate, but no West Wall Gate. The four outside walls of Ezekiel's imaginary Temple formed an overall structure of 500 × 500 cubits, or a square of about 875 feet long on each side.

After Ezekiel got the measurements of the East Gate from his guide, he saw the outer court and pavement with thirty chambers built next to the outer wall, and with a pavement running around the inside of the wall (40:5–27). Within the outer walls was another set of four walls—the inner walls—which formed the walls of the Temple area itself. These walls, like the outer walls, had three separate gates. The distance from the outer wall to the inner wall (40:17–19) around the Temple was 100 cubits or about 175 feet. Each outer wall gate—East, North, and South—had a corresponding set of gates in the inner wall. There was no West Gate because the

Temple faced toward the east and had no rear entrance (40:24–31).

We have now followed the prophet and his guide on their tour of the outer court of the Temple with its four walls, three gates, and rooms. I'm a bit of a carpenter myself, and I have a workshop with enough tools to build a small house. I'm vitally interested in my own little designs and blueprints, but I tend to either get lost or bored with Ezekiel's elaborate and exacting plans for his imaginary Temple. So I need to keep reminding myself that Ezekiel was a priest, and to him the Temple was the place that symbolized God's presence among His people.

To the prophet, the Temple was more than just a building, so we can understand that he wanted to see it constructed with the greatest precision and care. The Temple represented God's presence in the world. This is why Ezekiel spends so much time on the Temple details. He knew that worship is sensing and responding to the presence of God, and the Temple could focus that attention on God and keep it there. In a similar way Abraham Lincoln is just as alive to me today as when he walked the streets of Springfield, Illinois, because I have pored over his writings and life with loving care. And with equal intensity Thomas Jefferson comes alive to me as I tour his beautiful home at Monticello.

The Inner Court of the Temple

Having toured and described in minute detail the three gates of the outer wall, Ezekiel then did the same for the three corresponding gates in the inner wall (40:28–49). The South, East, and North Gates were identical to the outer gates in measurement, but they had eight steps instead of seven leading to the vestibule (40:32–37).

A number of tables were located by the vestibule of the North Wall Gate to be used for the sacrificial activity of the Temple. Here the priests slaughtered the animals and kept their butcher's tools (40:38–43). The priests were housed in two dormitories inside the inner court.

It's hard for me to be overly impressed with the symbolism of the structures that Ezekiel was describing. I've toured English, European, and Middle

Eastern castles, royal palaces, and cathedrals until I've come away numb with exhaustion and vowing that I would never set foot in another one. So I must keep reminding myself that for Ezekiel, the trained priest, each part of the structure had a religious function. As he moved from the outer court to the inner sanctuary, his sense of excitement grew. The very architecture of the Temple reminded him of the privilege and sanctity of the act of worship. While this Temple was real only in the mind of Ezekiel, it was real enough to make him believe that God would one day occupy His sacred house, and be among His chosen people.

I have gotten to the point where I can worship God almost any place—in a spare Quaker Meeting House, in a Rocky Mountain meadow at thirteen thousand feet, in a rented storefront mission station, or in a majestic cathedral like Westminster Abbey in London. As a Christian I know I can worship God anywhere at anytime. And yet there are certain places that will always be more sacred to me than others because they are associated with some special experience with God.

I may not share Ezekiel's longing to be in the Temple in Jerusalem, but I do share his feeling that God has been most real and close in certain hallowed places. Of course we agree with Stephen (Acts 6–8) that God does not dwell in houses made with hands (Isa. 66:1–2), and that the religious leaders of his day had turned the Temple ritual into an instrument of evil. Nevertheless, we sympathize with Ezekiel that a rebuilt Temple was a sign that God would once again be with His people.

The Ideal Symbolic New Temple

Having passed through the walled outer and inner courts, Ezekiel and his angelic guide came at last to the Temple itself (41:1–26). This imaginary building was a large one, rectangular in shape, with a single door in the East Wall. Inside were three rooms: a vestibule that led into a nave—the "holy place"— which then led into a small inner room, the "Holy of Holies." The "holy of holies" was a room that measured 20 by 20 cubits, or 35 feet square. In all, the Temple and its immediate area made a perfect square

(41:13–15). And the whole structure was set on a platform with steps leading up to it.

In his visionary visit the prophet gave a detailed description of the furnishings and decorations of the three interior rooms of the Temple. The three sets of doors were all double doors. In the nave was a table with provisions that symbolized God's presence, and the walls were panelled and decorated with designs of palm trees and cherubim. Everything about the Temple was designed to point to and protect the one small room, the "Holy of Holies." In real life only the high priest could enter this small inner room, and he could do that only once a year on the Day of Atonement. Of course the Creator of the universe was present everywhere, but this one little room—the Holy of Holies—symbolized His presence in an extraordinary way, and was looked upon with appropriate awe.

As Christians we keep coming back to the truth that Jesus has replaced the ancient Temple, that now we have direct access to the Heavenly Father without need of a Jewish high priest once a year, and that we can worship God anywhere in spirit and in truth. In the Gospel of John (2:13–25) we read that Jesus cleansed the Temple of the leaders to whom religion had become a business, and told them that His Father's house was in itself a claim to His Father's lordship (Psa. 69:9).

Jesus asserted that the faith which rested merely on signs, such as a building, and not on Him to whom they point is shallow and unstable (John 2:23–25). And then Jesus made an astounding claim—He was the new Temple of God. When the religious leaders challenged His right to drive them from the Temple, He responded: "Destroy this temple [the temple of his body], and in three days I will raise it up" (John 2:19). For the Christian, then, no holy building or holy land can ever be as sacred as they were to the Hebrew people before the coming of Jesus.

Rooms for the Priests

Ezekiel's final description of the visionary Temple dealt with two buildings which flanked the Temple on the north and south sides; they measured 100 by 50 cubits—about 175 by 87½ feet—and like the walls were three stories in height. These two service

In the magnificent vision described in Chapters 40 through 48, Ezekiel envisioned the rebuilt Temple and city of Jerusalem, the City of God. While we can't picture the city as he saw it, we catch some of its beauty today. At the left is a partial view of the eastern wall. At right is a view of a portion of the western wall and the colorful Dome of the Rock which occupies the site of the ancient Temple.

buildings were used by the priests when they ate their meals (42:1–20). They also served as storage places for offerings, and as changing rooms when the priests put on their priestly garments.

In Chapters 10–11 Ezekiel had seen God leave the Temple and Jerusalem. The symbolic Temple was no doubt a striking place, but until God returned to it, it was just another interesting building. A temple is not a temple without the living presence of God within it. Now Ezekiel had set the stage for the return of God's glory, and to this next episode of the vision we now turn.

God Returns to the Temple (43:1–12)

Up to this point in his vision, Ezekiel and his guide had been on a long tour of the restored Temple, examining and measuring its structure. Now the vision reached its climax as God returned to the building and spoke to the prophet from its innermost holy place.

In Ezekiel's vision God returned to the Temple through the same gate by which He left—the East Gate (43:1–5). This vision of God's return was extremely important to the prophet because the essence of the Hebrew religion was the personal relationship with God enjoyed by the Israelites.

Next, God spoke from the innermost sanctuary, indicating that He now was living in His symbolic home among His chosen people. God then set forth the conditions of His staying "at home": "Now let them put away their whoredom, and the carcases of their kings, far from me, and I will dwell in the midst of them for ever" (43:9). The lesson here is a simple one: the ground of our hope as Christians today, just as it was in the prophet's time, is the presence of the holy God among a holy people (Rev. 21:1–8). To know God is to know life; to drive God out of our life by our evil acts is to begin the slippery slide toward spiritual death.

Then Ezekiel was told to share his vision of the restored Temple with the Judean exiles (43:10–12). Then came the word that as soon as they were ready to submit in repentance to God, their restoration would begin. What a thrill of hope must have surged through the people as they listened to Ezekiel's descriptions.

Ezekiel then turned once again to describing the Temple. This time, however, he was mainly concerned to tell the Hebrew exiles how the Temple was to be used properly in worship.

How was this splendid but unoccupied building to be inaugurated and put to use? Ezekiel started with the altar, the very heart of the Temple (43:13–27). The altar was made of three large stone blocks—two pedestal blocks with an altar hearth on top—and located in the inner court. The altar was over twelve feet tall and had steps that led up its eastern side. Here sacrifices were offered which made possible an unbroken relationship with God (43:13–17).

Regulations For the Temple Service (43:12–46:24)

The Consecrated Altar

Seven days were to be set aside for consecration of the altar, and only on the eighth day were offerings to be made for the people (43:18–27). The purpose of the week of dedication was to let the people know that to approach God was an awesome responsibility not to be entered into flippantly or unadvisedly. Human evil had to be left at the foot of the altar before the gift of relationship could be experienced at the top of the altar.

Admission to the Sanctuary

Next, the prophet looked ahead to the time when the Jewish exiles would actually put the Temple into daily use, and he was concerned with laying down some functional rules (44:1–14). The East Gate was to remain closed to remind the people that God came through it as He returned to His Temple (44:1–3), and that He did not intend to leave again.

Much of Israel's past tragedy was due to the pagan influences that had been permitted in the Temple, so foreigners—gentiles—were not even to be allowed in the building (44:9). Unfortunately, this exclusivist attitude toward gentiles got distorted and came into great prominence during the time of Nehemiah and Ezra (440–20 B.C.) and continued on in the time of Jesus.

Since some of the Levites had turned to pagan worship in the past, they were not to be permitted to conduct Temple worship but were assigned various menial tasks (44:9–14). Instead, only the descendants of Zadok were allowed to function as priests.

The Holy Life of the Zadokite Priests

The Zadokite priests were descendants of Zadok, a man who served as high priest at the time of David. This family—the "sons of Zadok"—pretty much controlled the office of high priest from the tenth century until 171 B.C. And now only they were to serve at the Temple altar. Their whole life was to be dedicated to service to God. And they were to lead circumspect and holy lives, fitting for priests of the Lord (44:15–31).

These priestly descendants of Zadok had an awesome responsibility to be both spotless in inner motive and upright in outer conduct. In this way they were to serve as a constant reminder to the people that God demanded good moral conduct. In the restored Temple they were to combine the function of priests, prophets, and judges. Their responsibility as religious leaders of the people was awesome.

The Allocation of Land—Idealized Geography

Next, we are told that since the priests had no land of their own, God assigned a large block of territory to them (45:1–8)—an area of approximately sixty-four square miles. This land was to serve as a dwelling place for the Zadokite priests who conducted Temple worship; a specified allotment was for the Temple servants, and a specified area was allotted for the rebuilt Temple. In reading these verses we see that nothing was left to chance—their instructions were specific in every detail.

The symbolism behind this idealized geography as spelled out by the Ezekiel writer points up the perfection of the plan. The land, foursquare, was a perfect gift from a perfect God: The territory was perfectly square to reflect the character of God. Further, at the very heart of the restored land God's own special dwelling place was to be located. When the Jewish exiles returned to their homeland they were to come back as a *church,* a worshiping group gathered around the central core of God Himself from which all their blessings flowed. Ezekiel had reinterpreted what it meant to be the people of God. From here on, God was to be the focal point of their lives.

At this point let me again emphasize that Ezekiel knew that God was the awesome Creator of the universe and that He could never be confined to one locale or a million locales. He would have agreed with the statement: God is within all things, but not included; outside all things, but not excluded; and above all things, but not beyond their reach.

The Duties of the Prince

The prophet in verses 7 and 8 made reference to the land allotment to the future prince or ruler. Now he enlarges on the duties of the future ruler. In the past the rulers of Israel had frequently exercised their power corruptly, and Ezekiel lashed out at them with the typical fire of his earlier oracles (45:9–17). He still foresaw the establishment of a royal house in the restored land, but as things turned out in later years, it did not survive. But whether the restored people of Israel had a king or not, the prophet's message was still relevant: Rulers must rule according to the principles of justice and righteousness.

The princes were told to not engage in violence and oppression, and not to evict people from their land. In the past, the royal family, having no property, had often taken what they wanted. Years before, King Ahab, for example, had murdered Naboth for his vineyard (1 Kings 21). The rulers, known to change weights and measures to their own advantage, were now told to set honest standards for national commerce (45:9–12).

Ezekiel knew that in the past the rich and strong rulers had exploited the poor and weak and created a society of "haves" and "have nots." He demanded a return to justice because the new community could not thrive without it. Every citizen had to be given his "fair share of the pie" or their society would collapse again. In the words of India's Gandhi, "There is enough for the needy but not for the greedy."

The ruling princes were also responsible for making offerings to God on behalf of the people (45:13–17). In returning gifts to God the people would be constantly reminded of their need of a restored relationship with Him. God didn't really need their gifts, but they needed to have the experience of giving. In the past they had failed to learn that they were not a self-made people ("We did it all by ourselves"), and that the essence of living is giving ("Self-assertion is the way to self-fulfillment"). Their old illusions had to give way to new realities.

Worship in the Temple

Careful instructions are next given concerning worship in the restored Temple (45:18–25). The altar had already been consecrated (43:18–25), and a similar process was to be employed once a year for the Temple as a whole (45:18–20). The Feast of the Passover, which recalled their escape from slavery in Egypt centuries earlier, is described with detailed instructions as to the amount of offerings the prince is to make (45:21–25). They were to forever remember that they were a redeemed people. The Feast of

Tabernacles is mentioned in verse 25. This was a harvest festival, and its purpose was to remind them to give thanks to God for their daily bread.

Ezekiel was still not through speaking to the prince, the rulers, and he now lays down a variety of instructions about the conduct of worship (46:1–15). Each day the Temple was to be open for worship, but on Sabbaths and new moons (their calendar was based on a lunar system) the East Gate was to be opened so the prince might enter by the vestibule and take his place. From his appointed place the prince could observe his sacrifices being offered on the altar. Everything pertaining to the Temple worship was to be done decently and in order.

Worship Regulations for the Prince

As we read these verses, we get the feeling that Ezekiel had worked out in his own mind a healthy way to combine work and worship. How to relate the rhythm of daily work to a steady development of one's spiritual life has always, unfortunately, been a problem. Ezekiel knew that the people of Israel needed the great annual festivals—even as we need Christmas and Easter—but they also needed the disciplined simplicity of daily worship for inner spiritual health. Each day Ezekiel's ideal Temple was to be open, but every seventh day was to be a special day of worship.

As Christians we have come to see that while we have our special days and seasons of worship on our church calendars, in reality all of life is to be celebrated in worship and praise. We are beginning to realize the fallacy of the division of things "sacred" and "secular," for all of life for the Christian is sacred. Our work and our play, our times of busyness and our periods of leisure are all opportunities for worship and praise. Our God is not just the Lord of Sunday and church. Rather, He is our great Creator-God and has made all of our twenty-four hour days as opportunities for worship.

Ezekiel knew all too well how the rulers of Israel and Judah had abused the property rights of the ordinary citizen in the past years, so he now had a final word to the princes to safeguard the people from the

The Prince's Property

greed of the royal family. We read in these verses that the prince was given his own inheritance of land so there would be no need or excuse for him to confiscate the property of others. And the provision was made that even if the royal family leased some of their property, it would in due time revert back to them. The historical abuses of the property rights of the common people had wreaked havoc on the social structure of the northern kingdom of Israel leading up to its fall. And similar abuses had plagued the people of Judah leading up to the Babylonian conquest in 597–587 B.C.

The Temple Kitchens

As the prophet's vision continues, he was invited by his supernatural messenger to inspect the kitchens in the western side of the inner court of the Temple. Here the priests prepared the guilt and sin and cereal offerings. It was here, too, that their own food was prepared. And in the kitchen complex there were also four special kitchens in which the Levitical servants prepared food for the worshipers.

All of this preparation may seem very formal and elaborate to us, but it conveyed three simple ideas. First, it symbolized fellowship with God. Second, it was symbolic of the fellowship between the people of God. And third, it highlighted the simplest of all of God's marvelous provisions and blessings—food. Worship can be a grand public act, but it also includes something as ordinary as a meal shared in loving fellowship with friends. Over and over in the Gospels we read that Jesus shared a meal with friends. And among those events was the worship experience of the Last Supper with His disciples in the upper room the night before His death, and the breakfast of bread and fish on the shores of Galilee with His disciples after the resurrection.

Healing Waters—the River That Flowed from the Temple (47:1–12)

In Ezekiel's vision he next finds himself at the door of the rebuilt Temple. Here he sees a stream of water gushing out from under the threshold of the Temple and flowing east—"the waters came down from under the right side of the house [Temple], at the south side of the altar" (47:1b). The prophet and his supernatural guide followed the course of the stream for more than a mile. As the two walked along, they became aware of the fact that even though the stream was not fed by any tributaries, it miraculously got deeper and deeper (47:3–5). Then, as they turned back toward the Temple, Ezekiel saw that both sides of the stream were lined with luxuriant trees (47:7).

The prophet's guide told him that the ever deepening river flowed east toward the Dead Sea—that great salt lake some 1300 feet below sea level, into which the Jordan flowed and which had no outlet. Then, wonder of wonders, Ezekiel saw that the gushing stream cleared the waters of the Dead Sea until it was alive and teeming with fish. Furthermore, the stream watered the arid desert until it became luxuriant with fruit-bearing trees of all kinds (47:12). All of this reminds us of how the writer of the Book of Revelation picked up on Ezekiel's symbolism when he wrote, "And he shewed me a pure river of water of life, clear as crystal, proceeding out of the throne of God and of the Lamb. In the midst of the street of it, and on either side of the river, was there the tree of life, which bare twelve manner of fruits, and yielded her fruit every month" (Rev. 22:1–2). What a marvelous picture of God's ability to give life to the lifeless in both the Ezekiel and the Revelation verses.

This paradise, this new Garden of Eden, symbolized for Ezekiel God's transformation of the Babylonian exiles into a new and alive people. From now on God would be at the very center of their existence (the Temple), and His presence would flow out to transform their wilderness into a rich and spacious garden.

In this closing section of the Book of Ezekiel the prophet shifts to a legislative style of narrative. We recall that at the time of conquest Joshua had divided the Promised Land among the twelve tribes. However, Ezekiel envisioned quite a different arrangement and set of boundaries from Joshua's allocation.

The Division of the Restored Land (47:13–48:35)

In this description of position and boundaries (47:13–23) only the land west of the Jordan River was allotted to the twelve tribes. We have already seen

The Boundaries of the Land

95

Ezekiel's tendency to speak of the returned and restored exiles as being all of Israel rather than just the Judeans who had been in Babylon. In Ezekiel's optimism, he saw all twelve tribes returning to Palestine. So, in these verses he speaks specifically of the north, south, east, and west boundaries. But unlike the original layout, now all of the tribes are located west of the Jordan River and the Dead Sea, with each tribe occupying a strip of land that stretched from the Jordan or the Dead Sea to the Mediterranean.

The Allotment of the Land

We saw in an earlier oracle that Ezekiel had set aside a strip of land and divided it among the Levites, the Temple, the city of Jerusalem, and the prince or rulers (45:1–9). Now in Ezekiel's allocation diagram, this central "holy" area stretched from the Jordan to the Mediterranean and served as a divider, with seven tribes positioned to the north and five tribes to the south (48:1–29). Dan was the northernmost tribe. Then progressing south came Asher, Naphtali, Manasseh, Ephraim, Reuben, and Judah.

Next came the central strip which was set apart for God, the city, and the rulers. The land south between the Jordan River or the Dead Sea and the Mediterranean went to the tubes of Benjamin, Simeon, Issachar, Zebulon, with Gad on the southern boundary.

Now, it would be very easy for us to shrug our shoulders and say, "So what" to all of Ezekiel's detail here. His careful attention to size and shape, and his emphasis that each tribe's allotment of land was the same, and the orderliness of the arrangements was intended to focus the people's attention on God in a worshipful way. Their environment in exile was precarious in many ways, and they were constantly exposed to pagan influence and worship. Now the prophet wants them to see only their Creator-God.

You may remember that years ago Ted Malone had a radio show that came on early in the morning. On one of those programs he told about a shepherd in Idaho who made this request in a letter: "On the broadcast, will you strike the note A on the piano?" Then he went on to explain, "I'm a sheepherder on a lonely ranch here in Idaho. My only companion is an old violin, and it's out of tune. Would you please strike A so I can get back in tune?"

One day Ted Malone sounded A on the studio piano especially for the lonely sheepherder. Later he got a thank you note saying, "Now I'm in tune." Ezekiel with his visionary perfect land was trying to get his readers in tune with God so they could properly worship Him. And no amount of detail was too much in the accomplishment of that goal.

I recall so well one time of being with a group of students I had taken to Jerusalem. On Sunday we held our worship service at Gordon's Calvary near the Damascus Gate. At the conclusion of our service I served Communion, offering the bread and the cup to each one. Several years later I ran into one of those students, and the first thing he said to me was, "You served me Communion at Jesus' tomb." Of the hundreds of things we had done and seen on that trip, it was this simple act of worship that stood out in his mind. This was what Ezekiel wanted his countrymen to understand—the orderly worship of God must be central to their way of life.

New Jerusalem: The City of God

Ezekiel now concludes both his vision and his prophecy with a description of the City of God, the perfect city (48:30–35). The four city walls, all of the same length, would have twelve gates, one for each tribe. Once again we note the careful attention to detail, for the prophet tells us that the two tribes of Joseph, Ephraim and Manasseh would have just one gate between them. This would make it possible for a gate to be allotted to the descendants of Levi. This symbolizes the fact that all of God's people would be included, all would have access to Him.

We're also told here that the city would measure 18,000 cubits around—approximately six miles. But it would be known more for its holiness than for its beauty, size, or symmetry. And the city was to be named, "Yahweh-shammah"—"The Lord is there." It was God's presence and not size or architecture that would make the city stand out.

The name "The Lord Is There" stresses the entire message of Ezekiel's prophecy. The people of Israel had suffered in the past because the Lord was not "there." They were not punished *for* their sins, but *by* them. Because of sin, God had had to turn His back on Jerusalem, so it was sacked and burned by Nebuchadnezzar in 587 B.C. But now their future hope rested on the promise that "The Lord is there."

Ezekiel was an extraordinary man. He lived in a time when God seemed to have abandoned the sinking ship, and yet he is the most hopeful of all the prophets. While he didn't live to see the actual return and restoration of the people to their land, he saw it in his mind's eye decades before it happened. *Because he believed, he saw.* He didn't have to see to believe.

This is the marvelous lesson Ezekiel has for us who are late-twentieth-century Christians living in an often confusing and complex world. It is as we believe, that we see God at work in our world. It is as we believe that He can work in and through us.

Jesus, I believe; help thou my unbelief. AMEN.

WHAT THIS SCRIPTURE MEANS TO ME
Ezekiel 40–48

After reading these chapters of Ezekiel, I was left with several mental images—the splendor of the new temple, the glory of the Lord, offerings made upon the ritualistically cleansed altar, priests in their linen garments carrying out their ministerial duties and service, and water flowing between banks of fruit-bearing trees. These word pictures helped me to visualize what was described and what took place in Ezekiel's vision. But even more powerful than these images were the words which described God's commandments to Ezekiel and the people of Israel: Look, hear, set your mind, declare (40:4), teach, show, judge fairly and righteously, keep laws, obey ordinances (44:23), put away violence and oppression, and execute justice and righteousness (45:9). I believe that these words, declared by Ezekiel so long ago, should describe the behavior of each of God's people today.

A few months ago I became aware of an organization which honors people who "stick their necks out" for the common good. This foundation, called The Giraffe Project, is run by a married couple living near Seattle, Washington. In the five years of its existence, 252 "Giraffes" have been recognized and so-named because they were willing to take financial or social risks in order to help others. One such member gathers, repairs, and hands out gloves each winter to the homeless in New York. Another collects discarded potatoes from farmers and delivers them to the hungry. Still another has opened her home free of charge to pregnant, unmarried women.

These people, and many others, have received The Giraffe Project's certificate commending their courageous actions. In spite of facing the chance of losing a job or being ostracized by a community, these people performed good deeds of love, sacrifice, and service based on their faith, commitment, and deep convictions.

To this list of recognized Giraffes, I would add several of my own choosing:

- a Vietnam veteran who has become a father, teacher, and friend to more than five hundred troubled, orphaned, and abandoned boys in Guatemala
- a dedicated, self-giving man in Waco, Texas, who runs a food and clothing relief agency for the poor and hungry
- a bishop in South Africa who constantly risks punishment and imprisonment in order to promote justice and freedom from oppression

- a youngster who uses money he has earned from a paper route to purchase blankets for the "street people" in his city
- a woman who willingly offers love, affection, and care to unwanted babies born with the AIDS virus

All of these people are aware of situations around them which need particular attention—of wrongs which need to be corrected, of injustices which need to be rectified, of services which need to be performed, of care which needs to be given. I believe these people, and others throughout the world, are carrying out God's commandments to look, hear, and declare; to teach, show, and judge; to put away violence and oppression; to execute justice and righteousness.

I pray that God will grant me the courage, faith, and strength to follow His laws and ordinances in my daily life, to reach out to those in need, to be a voice for those unable to speak for themselves, to listen to the sounds of suffering around me, and to continually do what I can to make this world a better place.

Publisher's Introduction to Daniel

"There is a God in heaven that revealeth secrets [mysteries]." This was the God of history that Daniel served. This was the God who revealed the meaning of Nebuchadnezzar's dream; who was with Shadrach, Meshach, and Abednego in Nebuchadnezzar's crematorium; who closed up the mouths of the lions and spared Daniel; and who gave Daniel the interpretation of the handwriting on Belshazzar's wall.

The first half of the Book of Daniel gives us the fascinating story of four young Jewish men who as captives of a pagan king remained faithful to their God in the face of bitter adversity. In Chapters 1 through 6 the drama unfolds in living color. These stories of Daniel and his friends have inspired the people of God in every century by giving us models of faithful devotion to the one true God.

The second half of the Book of Daniel focuses on the screen of history. It includes a series of apocalyptic visions that speak of historic events and the parade of nations across the world's stage. The interpretation of these visions or dreams has stirred no end of speculation with the passing of time.

There are those interpreters of the Book of Daniel who date the writing around the time of Nebuchadnezzar (605–562 B.C.). Others place the actual writing of the book as we have it in the second century B.C., readily acknowledging that portions were handed down from an earlier time. Recognizing that there are responsible scholars on both sides of this question, for the purpose of our study here we have taken the position that it was written and brought together as we know it between 175 and 164 B.C.—a time of intense and bitter suffering under the maniacal rule of the Seleucid Antiochus IV.

The central message of the book is one of hope—it offered hope to the people of God who were its first readers. It has offered hope to God's faithful people throughout the centuries, and it offers hope to us as we move resolutely into the future. This hope is rooted in obedience to God irrespective of circumstances and events.

Further, this hope is based on the eternal truth that God is in charge of history. Tyrants and evil political ideologies have moved onto life's center stage from Antiochus IV to Hitler and Stalin and other like-minded despots. But in every case the God of history has intervened. Our twentieth century has witnessed the rise of communism and its threat to take over the world and force its atheistic philosophy on the entire human race. Doomsday prophets viewed the situation as hopeless.

But 1989 fouled up all the experts as we witnessed the breakdown of the communist system. In this we were reminded again that Daniel's God is still in charge of history. Our hope is rooted in Him.

Then, too, the Book of Daniel focuses the massive searchlight of hope on the truth that there is life after death—the resurrection of the body to a future life of meaning and purpose. In the Old Testament this is exclusive to the Book of Daniel.

Daniel's message pointed toward the coming Kingdom of God. This was his hope, and it is our hope.

Our trek through the Book of Daniel is an adventure of faith that is rich in dividends. In it we can say with Daniel, "Blessed be the name of God for ever and ever: for wisdom and might are his: And he changeth the times and the seasons: he removeth kings, and setteth up kings: he giveth wisdom unto the wise, and knowledge to them that know understanding" (2:20–21).

Preface to Daniel

The Book of Daniel is one of the best known books in the Bible. Even when I was a small boy with no knowledge of the Bible I had heard of the lion's den and the fiery furnace, and these stories captured my mind and stirred my imagination. I got the message that men of faith are imperiled because of their faith, but at the same time, saved by it.

As a young college student, I read the Book of Daniel for the first time and soon discovered that I was seriously handicapped in understanding it for two reasons: First, it belonged to a special type of literature—apocalyptic—which I had never heard of. Second, understanding it required a far more exact and detailed knowledge of the history of the ancient Near East than I possessed. And I quickly learned that it was one of the more difficult books of the Old Testament to understand.

After some initial hesitation, I resolved to gain a better understanding of apocalyptic literature and the history of the ancient Near East. My approach then, as now, is extremely conservative, that is, to first understand and then conserve the original intent of the author in its original context before making a present-day application.

A Special Type of Literature: Apocalyptic

When I first looked at this special class of writing that flourished in late Palestinian and early Christian times, I couldn't even spell the word *apocalyptic*. I learned, though, that it came from a Greek word meaning "to uncover, to reveal," and that it initially referred to the unveiling or uncovering of divine revelation in the form of a vision. It subsequently came to signify the books in which such visions were recorded. The Books of Daniel and Revelation belong to this kind of writing, and we've already been exposed to this type of literature in Ezekiel 1:1–3:27, etc. (see also Isa. 6:1–6; Joel 2:28–3:17; Zech. 12–14).

I discovered in my study that there are a number of Jewish apocalyptic writings, among which are the Book of Enoch, the Assumption of Moses, the Secrets of Enoch, the Apocalypse of Baruch, 4 Ezra, and the Sibylline Oracles. All of these books are esoteric in character, literary in form, symbolic in language, and pseudonymous in authorship; These books abound in visions, prayers, hymns; they reflect a fondness for numbers, ecstatic feelings, symbols, allegory, an emphasis on the end times, and they carry a sense of urgency. They preach that God will directly intervene in history to create a new and perfect age, and through symbolic images and visions show how God will have His will done on earth as it is in heaven.

These books also carry their own theological ideas, such as the truth that God is in control of history, that He is not indifferent to the world, that His power is equal to the needs of our time, and that only He can bring history to an end. They also teach that ethical and spiritual principles are eternal, there is life after death, and that God is always with us in a crisis. Then, too, these books have the pastoral aim to encourage the faithful in a time of danger and persecution. Written in times of persecution, they used a kind of spiritual code to make them "sealed books" (Dan.12:4) to those outside the circles of faith. In these books beasts generally represent nations or empires (today we have the Russian bear, the British lion, and the American eagle). And finally, I learned that these apocalyptic symbols are to be taken seriously but not literally.

In my study I found that the Book of Daniel shared these characteristics with apocalyptic literature, but that Daniel was strikingly different with a clearly defined message of its own. The Book of Daniel is much more restrained in its use of imagery, and refrains from flamboyant descriptions often found in other apocalyptic literature. Daniel also avoids the extravagance and fantastic imagination of these other books when it pictures the coming of God's kingdom and the signs of its appearing.

Prophecy in a New Idiom

In my first studies in the Book of Daniel and apocalyptic literature I found their central theme to be the coming of the kingdom of God at the End-Time. But this was exactly what the Old Testament prophets had always preached, and I was puzzled at this new expression of the old prophetic message.

From the very first the faith of Israel had looked toward the future fulfillment of God's promises. The people of Israel knew that they were involved in a great drama directed by God and moving toward a final consummation. In the time before the exile this hope found popular expression in the doctrine that on a certain day—the "Day of the Lord"—God would vindicate Israel by defeating her enemies and raising the chosen people to a position of prestige and blessing in the world. The great prophets challenged this view, rebuked Israel's national pride and complacency, and pled with the people to repent of their unfaithfulness to the covenant.

These prophets were concerned about the End-Time, but they saw it as a time after God had brought judgment upon His people. After the judgment God would renew His people in a New Age where the political schism of the Israelite monarchy would be healed, the blessings of fertility would be poured out abundantly, nations would cease to wage war, and the wilderness would blossom like a rose. Then Israel would live in the kingdom of God. The main concern of these prophets was how the future age impinged on the present.

But the exile (from 597–87 to 537 B.C.) brought a

shift of emphasis among the prophets. We have already seen this change in the prophet Ezekiel who stood on the boundary between the old national era and emerging Judaism. He preached the same seven themes as the other prophets, but he cast his message in unusual visions and strange symbolism. He looked beyond the exile and produced a diagram of the New Age drawn according to the pattern of a priestly utopia—the new Temple and the restored land. He saw this New Age being preceded by Gog from Magog attacking Jerusalem, but being defeated by the forces of righteousness in the final battle of history.

Ezekiel's drama of the overthrow of the symbolic Gog illustrates how apocalyptic literature tends to shift the prophetic emphasis upon God's judgment in the present through historical agencies—that is, the Babylonian king Nebuchadnezzar—to super-historical or cosmic proportions. This literature thought of God's enemies as more than flesh-and-blood; His enemies were a supernatural kingdom of evil led by God's archenemy Satan. God's final victory would take the form of the overthrow of Satan.

The new apocalyptic literature, then, was a new idiom for expressing the old prophetic message. It still said that God was king, that His kingdom was near, and that believers should be faithful under all pressures from the outside. Around 200 B.C. the Jewish people said that there was to be no new prophecy until the Messiah came to usher in the kingdom of God. A few years later, in 165 B.C., when the Jews ran into terrible trouble with the Greeks and desperately needed a prophetic message from God, apocalyptic literature stepped into the gap to supply that message. It is not surprising that in our day, when many people have suffered cruelly at the hands of demonic forces, the apocalyptic messages of the Books of Daniel and Revelation have spoken with new relevance.

The Middle East Before 165 B.C.

The backdrop of the Book of Daniel covers a stretch of time of almost four and a half centuries. In my early studies in the book I had to get acquainted with the history of the Jews and their contacts with the empires of Babylon, Medo-Persia, Greece, Syria (the Seleucidae), and Egypt (the Ptolemies). Rome stood just offstage, so I had to know something of Rome's early history as well.

The Book of Daniel moves with ease back and forth over this history, but its focus of interest is upon the successors to Alexander the Great (336–323 B.C.), and more especially upon one Seleucid king, Antiochus IV, who was called Epiphanes. The dates of Antiochus Epiphanes are 175–164 B.C., and one of my best sources for his immediate background was 1 Maccabees 1:1–4:60 in the *Apocrypha.*

After the death of Alexander the Great his general Seleucus took power in Syria and founded the Seleucid dynasty, while his general Ptolemy assumed power in Egypt and founded the Ptolemaic dynasty. Between these two centers of political power, Palestine once again became a land bridge for commerce or military conquest. Under the Egyptians (Ptolemies) the Jews were free to practice their own religion, but this situation changed when the Syrians (Seleucids) began to rule Palestine following the battle of Paneas in 198 B.C. Jewish life and faith came under attack when Antiochus IV ascended the throne.

In my studies I found that Antiochus IV had two consuming ambitions, one political and the other cultural. He wanted to conquer Egypt with his army, and he wanted to Hellenize—impose Greek culture and religion upon—the whole Middle East. The Jews stood in the way of both his ambitions. He passed through Judah on his military campaign to Egypt where he suffered a defeat. On his way back home he turned on the Jews as scapegoats for his setbacks.

Antiochus set up a program to Hellenize the Jews, and many of them offered him no resistance. Hellenism had already made an impression on the Middle East by the time Alexander died in 323 B.C. Greek was spoken everywhere, stadia had been built in many cities and seasonal Greek games were held, Greek clothing was worn, Greek manners were imitated, and the Hellenistic spirit exercised a major influence on religious ideas and values.

Early in his reign Antiochus, who believed he was the god Zeus incarnate, agreed to sell the office of the high priest in Jerusalem to the highest bidder, and he found priests who were willing to collaborate with him. This action struck horror into Jewish hearts and caused great revulsion to Jewish minds, and a hard core of loyal Jews began to resist him. On his way back through Palestine after his unsuccessful military campaign in Egypt in 168 B.C., Antiochus sacked the Temple and installed a high priest who was willing to refashion the Jewish heritage into the form of Syro-Hellenistic religion.

As a part of his program, Antiochus made it a capital offense for Jews to circumcise a baby, to own a copy of the Jewish Law, to keep the Sabbath, and to make an offering to God. He consecrated the Jerusalem Temple to Zeus and sacrificed swine upon its altars. He set up Greek altars throughout Judah, and before the eyes of the local citizens a designated Jew was commanded to sacrifice a pig to Zeus Olympus. This program was the spark which lighted the fires of rebellion. Antiochus desecrated the Temple on December 25, 168 B.C., and exactly three years later, on December 25, 165 B.C., the Jews rededicated the liberated Temple.

Rebellion against Antiochus began in the small village of Modein in 168 B.C. A renegade Jew was about to make the required gentile sacrifice when Mattathias, a local priest, struck down the renegade and the Greek officer who was the king's representative (1 Macc. 2:1–28). Mattathias led the Maccabean revolt for about a year until his death, when Judas, one of his five sons, assumed leadership. Judas led a very effective guerrilla warfare against the Greeks (1 Macc. 2:65–3:60) and was nicknamed "Maccabee," the "hammerer." A year after the Temple was cleansed and reconstituted for regular worship (1 Macc. 4:52–61) Antiochus died.

Judas led such a hard-hitting campaign against the enemy, both Jewish assimilationists and Greek Syrians, that what began as a resistance movement flared into a full-scale war. With Rome's intervention in eastern affairs, the zealous Maccabees were able to achieve a century of independence that lasted until the coming of the Roman ruler, Pompey, to Jerusalem in 63 B.C.

When I began my teenage first study of the Book of Daniel, I assumed it had been written in the sixth century B.C.—605 B.C. and following—during the Babylonian exile by Daniel himself, one of the Jewish exiles. The book portrays Daniel doing his work as the Babylonian empire was breaking up and the new empire of Persia was emerging. This is the impression that most people get on first reading the Book of Daniel, and I took it to be the memoirs of a Hebrew hero who lived in trying times and who had visions of a better day. If you, as a reader of this book, wish to hold to that traditional dating, I trust that you will be open to the approach I take. It is my belief that the Book of Daniel was written around 165 B.C.; however, I recognize the presence of earlier material (Chapters 1–6). This is the widely accepted position among most of today's scholars.

The Writing of the Book of Daniel

Daniel was an authentic hero of the Babylonian exile. We saw in our study of the Book of Ezekiel that Nebuchadnezzar in 597 B.C. transported into exile three groups of citizens to hold as hostages: King Jehoiachin and his family; Ezekiel and the priestly class; and the landed gentry. Daniel was most likely a part of the landed or wealthy class that went into exile.

Daniel the Hero

Daniel rose to a position of power under King Nebuchadnezzar, but he never forgot that he was a servant of the one true God. His faith in God landed him in all kinds of trouble, but that same faith saw him through his troubles. His exploits for God became a model example for the Judean exiles, and stories of his feats were lovingly passed down from one generation of Jews to another. He became in fact and legend one of the great heroes of the past. In chapters 1–6 of the Book of Daniel we have only six of the many stories about this grand warrior for God.

Shortly after the Maccabean revolt started, an unknown writer composed the Book of Daniel. Undoubtedly he was one of the pious Jews, a member of the Hasidim, who felt a revulsion for Hellenism and the tyranny of Antiochus. His purpose in writing was to rekindle the faith of the Jews and keep them loyal in the face of persecution and death. He set forth the theology of the Maccabean revolution, and the Book of Daniel has rightly been called "the Manifesto of the Hasidim."

In my opinion, then, the author of Daniel was a Jew, writing in the second century and in the name of a Hebrew exile who lived four hundred years before. His purpose was not to deceive his readers but to write in the name of an ancient worthy long honored in the traditions of Israel and thus tie together Chapters 1–6 and Chapters 7–12. As we have seen, this pseudonymity of authorship was a common practice in apocalyptic literature. The Book of Daniel may have actually been written in the second century B.C., but page after page of it had been composed in the centuries before.

As indicated earlier there are those interpreters who believe that the Book of Daniel was written during the Babylonian exile. And they regard it as a prophetic preview of several centuries of future history, and, indeed, of God's program for a future time. In our study of the Book of Ezekiel we saw that, although the prophets looked to the future, they were concerned primarily with the meaning of the present.

The Main Themes in Daniel

The author of Daniel wrote for the crisis of his own day, and he wrote to people who were being killed for their faith. He stressed several themes in his book. First, the sovereign Lord God is in control of all history. Each succeeding empire must be viewed from the standpoint of God and His moral requirements, for He is the ruler of all nations. Mighty monarchs are allowed to rule only by His permission, and His faithful people will be completely vindicated at the end of history. Since God governs the cosmos, the righteous are to take heart in the face of evil. In His sovereignty He can watch over youths in a fiery furnace, extricate the faithful from lions' dens, and drive the great ones to madness.

Second, the way of loyal faith is the right way, and faith is the ground of assurance of God's ultimate victory. Greek cultural claims are false, and men of faith will not conform to the latest fashion or follow the customs of the day. Three men under the threat of the fiery furnace still would not submit to the degradation of heathen practice, and their confidence in God brought them through unscorched.

Third, the author of Daniel gives "salvation" a new and broader understanding. Of course, God would rescue individuals, as seen in Chapters 1–6, but this view was not new. However, Daniel's wider view saw God's kingdom intruding into history and replacing all other kingdoms. In Daniel a time of destruction would precede the establishment of God's everlasting kingdom in which the martyrs would be vindicated. Salvation transcended the political limits and destiny of Israel or any other national boundary. This concept of God's universal rule was later incorporated in New Testament thought where Jesus and the apostles gave it its fullest expression.

Fourth, the author revises the older view of the political Messiah and pictures instead a supernatural Messiah, the son of man (7:13–14). The coming kingdom will not be a political reality, but a divine victory transcending and transfiguring the ordinary realities of history. The Seleucids and Ptolemies vie for power, but God's kingdom moves to a higher plane (Chapter 12). God's kingdom is not a human kingdom or a utopia of any social planning. Only God can create it by His miraculous power and in His own good time. For the full realization of this kingdom Christians continue to hope and pray.

Fifth, the author of Daniel teaches that there is to be a general resurrection of the dead (12:2). This is one of the few passages in the Old Testament to present the belief in a life after death. This doctrine, one of the great contributions of apocalyptic literature, was late in coming. The resurrection of the body, that is, the self, is portrayed as happening at the End-Time when God squelches the powers of evil.

Sixth, evil is a reality to be taken seriously. Evil always has a human face, and this human idolatry corrupts the created order and turns the work of God into demonic powers. Evil is a mystery: It is alluring, but its good appearance is deceptive. Evil is self-destructive: Satan carries a lash, but is on a leash held by God.

The important thing for us now is to move ahead in our study of Daniel with an open mind and prayerful attitude. There is a powerful message here for us because this book also belongs to our times. God's message can come to us even in this unusual— to us—apocalyptic form.

Chronological Outline

Date	Event
623 B.C.	Ezekiel born
605 B.C.	Assyria destroyed by Babylon; beginning of Nebuchadnezzar's reign
597 B.C.	Jehoiachin surrenders to Babylon and is deported; Ezekiel and the youth Daniel go into exile
593 B.C.	Ezekiel receives his call to prophesy
587 B.C.	Jerusalem captured and the Temple is destroyed
573 B.C.	Ezekiel's vision of the Temple; his last recorded prophecy
539 B.C.	Accession of Cyrus the Persian to the throne of Babylon; Jews prepare to return to Palestine
440–20 B.C.	Nehemiah and Ezra
323 B.C.	Death of Alexander the Great, the Greek
323–198 B.C.	Ptolemaic (Egyptian) control of Palestine
198 B.C.	Beginning of Seleucid (Syrian) control of Palestine
175–164 B.C.	Reign of Antiochus Epiphanes
175–171 B.C.	Jason, high priest
171–162 B.C.	Menelaus, high priest

168 B.C.	Leadership by Judas Maccabeus
164 B.C.	Restoration of the Temple and religious privileges
63 B.C.	Pompey, the Roman, captures Jerusalem

LESSON 5
Daniel 1–3

Faith in God:
Its Rewards and Dangers

Jesus, Help me to faithfully observe Your Word; let my life be guided by Your precepts. AMEN.

Nebuchadnezzar had conquered Jerusalem in 597 B.C., pillaged the Temple, and taken hostages to Babylon. The Book of Daniel begins with a series of short stories (Chapters 1–6) about four of these young Jewish captives. They were in an alien culture with a strange government, a foreign people, and a pagan, polytheistic religion. They were in the very place where wickedness had been exiled and had made its home (cf. Zech. 5:8), where the gods Bel or Marduk (Isa. 46:1) now possessed the sacred vessels of the Jerusalem Temple, and they were being asked to work for the Babylonian government. What were they to do? Could they remain loyal to the God of Israel under the pressure of such an alien culture? Their decision would become an example to all the exiled Jews.

I think there is good reason to believe that the author of the Book of Daniel retold the stories of these four Jewish young men to encourage the people of his own time to hold fast to their faith in the midst of their own alien culture. Just as Daniel and his

A Wisdom Story of Daniel and His Friends: How Faithful Observance of the Law is Rewarded (1:1–21)

friends stood firm against all pressures and were rescued by God, so the Jews should stand firm against the Greek culture of Antiochus Epiphanes and God would deliver them. They could see that God had dealt with Nebuchadnezzar in the past, and so He would handle Antiochus in the present. For the loyal and the brave, God's support was certain and His wisdom was always available.

The early Christians in the great Roman empire felt the same pressures as the writer of the Book of Daniel to conform to an alien culture, but they, too, were determined not to let the world squeeze them into its mold (Rom. 12:1). Jesus had already told them that they might be betrayed, arrested, and beaten (Mark 13:9), but they were to hold steady and be the salt of the earth and the light of the world.

One Christmas I was visiting former classmates in a Middle Eastern country where any formal, organized Christianity was actively discouraged. My friends could worship God in their own home or in the back room of a bookstore owned by a Christian friend, but church buildings were outlawed by the government. Believe me, that was not the most peaceful Christmas I have ever had—I was too alert to possible danger—but it was certainly memorable and meaningful as I tried to worship the "Prince of Peace" under those adverse conditions.

The stories of Daniel can fortify the faith of God's people today and strengthen our resolve just as they did when they were first written. During the opening days of the Second World War in 1940, Winston Churchill challenged his people to bravery with these ringing words: "Let us . . . brace ourselves to our duty, and so bear ourselves that, if the British Empire and its Commonwealth last for a thousand years, men will still say: 'This was their finest hour.' " A time of stress may well come when we will have to brace ourselves for our service to God as did the Hebrews who first read the Daniel story.

Four Friends in a Foreign Land

Our story opens with a description of the situation confronted by Daniel and his three friends in exile (1:1–7). In 597 B.C. Nebuchadnezzar had carried off Daniel, Ezekiel, and the elite of Jerusalem to Babylon as hostages. Then, ten years later in 587 B.C. Nebuchadnezzar and his army had destroyed Jerusalem by fire and many more of the people of Judah were taken into exile, and about five thousand of them that survived the march ended up at Tel-Abib.

Daniel and the first group apparently represented the most cultured, intelligent, and religious elements among the Judean exiles (2 Kings 24:14–16; Jer. 29:1). They were not slaves but foreign captives who enjoyed a fair measure of freedom. This elite group of hostages built and lived in their own houses in a self-contained community and stayed in touch with their kinsmen back in Judah. But the second group of exiles in 587 B.C. were most likely treated harshly and forced to work as convicts on government building projects. And after Nebuchadnezzar died in 562 B.C., their condition probably worsened.

Nebuchadnezzar was succeeded by his son Evil-Merodach (562–560 B.C.) who in turn was murdered by Neriglissar (560–556 B.C.). Neriglissar's short reign was marked by rebellion and conspiracies. By this time the Babylonian empire had started to skid into a rapid decline.

Neriglissar was succeeded by his son Labashi-Marduk who was murdered after a reign of only nine months. Next, Nabonidus of Harran was crowned king (556–539 B.C.). Nabonidus was evidently an effective military leader and a very religious man who was deeply devoted to the moon god Sin. It is likely the Jews experienced harsh times during his reign. Finally, the armies of Nabonidus suffered defeat by Cyrus the Persian in 539 B.C. Without doubt, the rapid turnover of kings during Babylon's decline brought about troubled times for the Jews, not unlike the times of foreign oppression experienced by the first readers of the Book of Daniel.

Those early readers in 165 B.C. would have recognized the parallel between the period of Nebuchadnezzar/Nabonidus and the Greek Antiochus IV (175–164 B.C.) Even as the Babylonians had desecrated the Temple centuries before when Jerusalem was destroyed, so Antiochus IV had committed a similar sacrilege in their time.

It seems quite likely that the author of the Book of

Daniel, by recalling the heroic stories of the Babylonian period, hoped to encourage his countrymen to stand fast in their faith against Antiochus IV. He wanted them to believe that God would soon come to their rescue even while he wanted them to trust God to give them wisdom and strength to cope with their persecution.

Daniel and His Friends Are Selected to Serve

Next we read that Daniel and his friends were recruited into the Babylonian bureaucracy and given a prescribed course of training (1:3–5). It was a common practice for rulers to choose the well-favored from their prisoners of war for special training and service, and Ashpenaz, the chief of Nebuchadnezzar's eunuchs, was ordered to institute such a program. To qualify for this special position the young men had to come from aristocratic families and be gifted with knowledge and good looks. In addition the young men were to undergo a three year indoctrination process to put them in a high office that gave them power with gods and men. And as a part of their training they learned the Sumerian tongue and the complicated cuneiform script (1:4).

The word *Chaldean* originally meant the royal family of Nebuchadnezzar, but it later came to mean a class of influential Babylonian priests who were famous for their learning in astrology, divination, and magic—in all but two instances this priestly meaning is the one implied in the Book of Daniel. The author of Daniel tells of this training to demonstrate that the Babylonian wisdom cannot even begin to compare with the wisdom given by God to Daniel and his friends.

Having sketched this general background, the author introduced the four main Jewish characters. They were Daniel, Hananiah, Misha-el, and Azariah. All four were from the tribe of Judah, and had names which contained some form of the name of Israel's God. It is likely they were unhappy with the decision of the chief eunuch to rename them because their new names contained or had reference to Babylonian gods. Daniel became Belteshazzar, which means "may Bel protect the life of the prince." Hananiah became Shadrach, which is a form of the god-name Marduk.

Misha-el became Meshach, a name apparently associated with Marduk. Azariah became Abednego, a name meaning the servant of the god Nebo (1:6–7).

To the Hebrews a name connoted the character of a person. To change a person's name by force was to tamper with his or her innermost being and possibly endanger that person's relationship to God. Even in the twentieth century a name can still imply character. This certainly became the case with Rosa Parks—when she sat down that day in the segregated bus in Montgomery, Alabama, the rest of the world stood up.

Almost immediately the four young Jews were confronted with a major decision. As a part of their preparation process, they were to be served the very

The Dietary Dilemma—Food and Faith

Among the ruins in Babylon is this roadway which dates to the time of Daniel. It is believed this is a road on which he likely walked.

same food and drink that graced the king's table. But for them, this meant a violation of their dietary laws (1:8–16). Early in Hebrew history definite instructions were given concerning their food (Deut. 12:23–28; 14:3–21; Lev. 11). It was these dietary rules that came to symbolize their whole way of life—that set them apart from their pagan neighbors.

For Daniel and his three friends to eat the king's food would have been a direct violation of Jewish law. For them, it was "unclean" and not fit to eat. When Daniel suggested to the "prince of the eunuchs" that they be served simpler foods which were prepared according to Jewish custom, he was reminded they were all in serious danger if the king's instructions weren't followed. Quite naturally he was more concerned for himself—"ye make me endanger my head [I may lose my head]" (1:10).

In response, Daniel was the epitome of tact and wisdom as he suggested they be put to the test for ten days. During the test period they would eat nothing but vegetables and drink water. Then at the end of the test period their appearance could be compared with the other young men who had followed the king's instructions (1:11–13).

Next we read that Daniel's suggestion was agreed to, and the Daniel writer says, "And at the end of ten days their countenances appeared fairer and fatter in flesh than all the children [the other young men] which did eat the portion of the king's meat" (1:15). In fact, they looked so much better that Melzar, the head eunuch, supplied the food they could eat without any further question (1:16).

Now, once again the first readers of the Book of Daniel would have found comfort in this story. During the Maccabean revolt they were severely persecuted for holding rigidly to their ancient dietary laws. In fact, it was at this time that Antiochus IV forced the Jews on penalty of death to eat swine's flesh.

Many of the Jews died rather than knuckle under and betray their religious dietary principles. The Apocrypha book of 2 Maccabees tells the story of a mother and her seven sons who were tortured and executed by order of Antiochus IV for refusing to eat pork (7:1–42) because it was considered unclean and in violation of their religious principles. To those second century B.C. Jews the story of the faithfulness of Daniel and his three friends several hundred years before would have been a great encouragement. They learned from the Daniel story that God's food laws must be maintained and that God would reward those who were loyal to Him.

It is interesting how some seemingly insignificant thing—such as food—or some trivial event can highlight our faith in God. In his autobiography, Phil Donahue told of an experience of his television crew in the Appalachian community of Holden, West Virginia. They were covering the rescue attempt of thirty-eight trapped miners. When the tired rescuers and the men finally emerged from the mine, a local preacher said to the tearful relatives, "Let us pray." Following the prayer they all joined hands and sang, "What a Friend We Have in Jesus."

Mr. Donahue said that was a beautiful scene, but his cameras missed the picture because of technical difficulties. Some time later, around 2:30 in the morning, he finally got his equipment working and approached the pastor with the request that he repeat the earlier scene for the cameras. The minister politely refused.

Phil Donahue was shocked that anyone would turn down the opportunity to be on network television. But then he said that the preacher's refusal to "show biz" for Jesus was one of the greatest demonstrations of moral courage that he had ever encountered.

Indeed, it was moral and spiritual courage of the highest order that prompted Daniel and his three companions to abide by the ritualistic dietary laws God had laid out for their ancestors centuries earlier. But, then, as you will remember, Jesus, when He was condemned by the Pharisees for not holding to the ancient dietary provisions, put ritual purity in proper perspective when He said, "There is nothing from without a man, that entering into him can defile him" (Mark 7:15).

But Jesus didn't stop there, for He went on to teach that morally accepted attitudes are what a pure and

121

holy God is really interested in. God wants us to distinguish between outer legal observances and inward moral and spiritual growth. Again and again Jesus drove this point home, but the disciples and the early church were slow to learn the lesson that the "letter of the law" must give way to the spirit (Acts 10:9–16). It was this which for years in the first century of our Christian era created tensions between Jewish Christians and the gentile believers (Gal. 2:11–13; Col. 2:16). Finally, the Apostle Paul gave the best guidance on the matter when he observed that legal requirements are nothing in themselves, but a mature and loving Christian will be very sympathetic to a fellow Christian who still has a tender conscience over such matters (Rom. 14:14, 21). The church should be such a loving fellowship that a mature believer should meet a "weaker" believer halfway (1 Cor. 10). When the story of Daniel and his three friends is transferred to a Christian context, the legal requirements are superseded by moral response and mutual love.

Success and Blessing: the Reward of Loyalty to God

The point of the food story in Daniel is to show how faithful observance of the Law is rewarded by favorable standing in society and chances of promotion; that is, God looks after His own (1:17–21). In the case of Daniel and his friends, they received the gifts of physical fitness, attractiveness, and superior mental ability. By God's grace they soon beat the Babylonian caste of sages at their own game of secret traditions. To know is not to be wise, but to know how to use knowledge is to have wisdom. And Daniel was given the added gift of properly interpreting dreams. Even the king recognized the superiority of their wisdom was from God Himself, and the four young men were learning that God supported the loyal and the brave.

The author of the Book of Daniel was supremely confident that God would reward the faithful. But this is no easy triumphalism, because as we will see the four heroes had some terrible suffering to endure. The story of Joseph has a parallel here also, because he went through years of pain before he became Prime Minister of Egypt (Gen. 50:20). Then Job demonstrated that the righteous are not immune to sorrow. And Jesus promised His disciples a "hundredfold" reward (Mark 10:30) but only "with persecutions." The Christian religion is not a good luck charm to good fortune. Neither Daniel nor Jesus preached a cheap "gospel of success." But as we take up our cross daily and follow Christ, we know that God is at work in all kinds of circumstances to bring about ultimate good to those who love Him.

We can be certain that God is with us to bless us even in our times of pain and suffering, as He was with Daniel. The ability to see or interpret this was a gift from God to Daniel. Indeed, the ability to see beyond appearances to reality is not something we can acquire on our own; rather, it is a gift of the Spirit. The Apostle Paul got this into the right perspective when he wrote, "But the natural man receiveth not the things of the Spirit of God: for they are foolishness unto him: neither can he know them, because they are spiritually discerned" (1 Cor. 2:14).

I once read the story of Libby Fisher, a very special teacher who taught school in Connecticut for forty-five years. It was said of Miss Fisher that she was familiar with every trick of the "little monsters" and with the special pleading of their parents, and yet she still loved teaching. She was described as a person who always looked as if something wonderful was about to happen and that she had private word ahead of time. I strongly suspect that description fits Daniel as well—even as it should be descriptive of each of us, because with the Apostle Paul "we know that all things work together for good to them that love God, to them who are the called according to his purpose" (Rom. 8:28).

The point of the marvelous wisdom story told in this part of our Scripture lesson is that all of the divinations, incantations, and magical formulae of the pagan world's wisdom was no match for the wisdom God gives His faithful followers.

A Wisdom Story of Nebuchadnezzar's Dream—A Comparison of Human Wisdom with God's Wisdom (2:1–49)

Pagan Wisdom versus God's Wisdom

We learn now in the Daniel story that King Nebuchadnezzar was plagued with some troubling dreams which were keeping him awake at night (2:1). This was serious because the people of the ancient Near East attached great importance to dreams and their mysterious content. Consequently, it was common practice in those days for kings to retain a large contingent of religious functionaries and magicians whose primary task was to interpret dreams. This was true of Nebuchadnezzar, and the Daniel writer now says, "Then the king commanded to call the magicians, and the astrologers, and the sorcerers, and the Chaldeans, for to shew the king his dreams" (2:2). When they were all assembled, they asked the king to tell them the dream.

At this point the story has a strange twist. The king had forgotten the content of the dream. And with that, he told them they must reconstruct his dream and then interpret it for him. What an impossible assignment! But they were also warned as to what would happen if they failed, "ye shall be cut in pieces, and your houses shall be made a dunghill." But if they succeeded, they would receive rich rewards and high honors (2:5–6).

Obviously, the magicians and astrologers and the sorcerers and the Chaldeans were between a rock and a hard place. They knew there was no way under the sun they could actually recover the content of the dream, and they tried to explain this to the troubled king. We can almost imagine their anguish as in desperation they said, "It is a rare thing that the king requireth, and there is none other that can shew it before the king, except the gods, whose dwelling is not with flesh" (2:11).

We next read that in a fit of irrational anger Nebuchadnezzar pronounced doom on "all the wise men of Babylon" by issuing a decree that they should be killed (2:12–13). And, apparently, it wasn't until the decree was issued that Daniel knew about what was happening. In the meantime he had completed his three years of preparation and was now classified among the wise men of the country. But Daniel's wisdom was quite different from that of the Babylonian so-called wise men. He had the gift of spiritual insight and knew that God was in control of people and nations. Daniel's insights were not based on native ability, technical skills, chance, or chicanery.

Rather, he knew how to preserve the traditions of the past and use them to strengthen God's people in their time of suffering.

The New Testament writers saw in the Book of Daniel and the Old Testament wisdom books—Job, Proverbs, Ecclesiastes, and certain psalms—a perfect background for Jesus Christ. In Christ they saw the fulfillment of all wisdom (Eph. 3:10). The Luke writer stated the Christ was the wisest of the wise (Luke 11:31), and the Apostle Paul saw in Jesus Christ a wisdom far greater than any pagan wisdom (1 Cor. 1:20–24).

Politeness, Prayer, and Praise

In the next scene, Daniel, upon hearing about the king's decree, questions Arioch, the captain of the king's guard, about what is going on. And upon hearing the story, he asks for an audience with the king (2:14–16). But first Daniel returned to his home and asked his three friends to pray with him for God's mercy and help in revealing the mystery of the dream. The author of the Book of Daniel wanted his readers to see that Daniel's need for wisdom and prayer was a model for helping them through the crises they were enduring under Antiochus. Like Daniel, their spiritual ancestor, their piety was not dependent on being in the Temple or synagogue— God would be with them wherever they were, and their intercessory prayers would prove that their God was indeed the source of all wisdom.

Following their time of urgent prayer, the secret of the king's dream was revealed to Daniel who then offered a beautiful prayer of praise and thanksgiving to God who had revealed "the deep and secret things" and had given him the wisdom he needed to meet the present crisis (2:19–23). I have to believe that the author of the Book of Daniel wanted his Jewish readers to see in this prayer a clear call to trust in God's guiding hand. Both Nebuchadnezzar and Antiochus IV might arrogantly imagine they were running the world, but the wise worshiper of God knew that He alone is the source of all knowledge and power.

As we move along through this story, we can't help but see the parallel with the drama of Joseph in

Egypt (Gen. 41). You recall that young Joseph was given the interpretation of the Pharaoh's dream. The Joseph story illustrated the truth that God was in control of the day-to-day affairs of people. But we will see in the Daniel story that God is in control of the century-by-century rise and fall of empires and nations, and that in His time He will bring all of history to a dramatic conclusion. The author of the Book of Daniel underlines the point that pagan cultures, for all of their vaunted wisdom, cannot interpret life's mysteries. Indeed, pagan and worldly philosophies are so bankrupt that they cannot interpret the present—let alone the future.

Daniel, the Interpreter of Dreams

Daniel, with supreme confidence in God, asked Arioch to suspend the order of execution of all of Babylon's wise men as he would comply with the king's wishes. When Daniel was presented to the royal court, he reiterated the truth that no human could recall and interpret the king's dream. However, the God of the Jews had revealed to him the dream and its meaning, which involved God's rule over all the affairs of humankind (2:24–30).

Daniel's use of the expression "what shall be in the latter days" (2:28) is a phrase that had long been used by the prophets to describe the coming messianic age when God would move history toward its conclusion. We see then that Daniel's interpretation of the dream carried the message of the coming kingdom of God and how the Lord would deal with the nations of the world in preparation for His coming kingdom. In the New Testament Jesus is seen as the supreme Interpreter of the mysteries of God, and there God is pictured as redeeming not only the nations of the world but all of the created universe (Rom. 8:19).

Next, Daniel tells the king the content of his forgotten but troubling dream (2:31–35). Catch the drama of that moment, "Thou, O king, sawest, and behold a great image. This great image, whose brightness was excellent [dazzling], stood before thee; and the form thereof was terrible [fearful, awesome]. This image's head was of fine gold, his breast and his arms of silver, his belly and his thighs of brass, His legs of iron, his feet part of iron and part of clay. Thou sawest [watched] till that a stone was cut out without hands, which smote [struck] the image upon his feet that were of iron and clay, and brake them to pieces. Then was the iron, the clay, the brass, the silver, and the gold, broken to pieces . . . and the stone . . . became a great mountain'' (2:31–35).

Daniel then proceeded to interpret the dream for Nebuchadnezzar (2:36–45). The metals in the colossus represented earthly kingdoms in descending order of worth, with the head of gold representing Nebuchadnezzar and the Babylonian empire. The king was told that his kingship and authority had been given to him in trust by God who alone established rulers and kingdoms. But now a second kingdom (silver) would rise and take his place. Daniel didn't identify the silver kingdom, but elsewhere in the Book of Daniel the indications are that it was the Median empire.

If this interpretation so far is correct, the "brass" kingdom would be Persia. And, finally, the fourth kingdom of iron would be Greece. But the Grecian empire, like a mixture of iron and clay, would prove too brittle to stand for long. The hostility between the Ptolemies of Egypt (the clay) and the Seleucids of Syria (the iron) as well as the intermarriage of races and cultures encouraged by Alexander the Great and his successors would spell its doom.

The author of the Book of Daniel focused on the fourth kingdom because it was the one that would be shattered ultimately by God's new kingdom—the supernatural stone. He looked to that time when Antiochus IV met his doom and the Jews would be rescued and share in God's rule, which would last forever.

Now, there is no precise hint in Daniel's vision as to timing. We do know that the various kingdoms or empires represented in Daniel's vision came and then passed off the scene. We know, too, that God's kingdom emerged into reality in the life, death, and resurrection of Jesus Christ and that at some future time, history, as we understand it, will culminate with the return of Jesus. At that time, Daniel's vision will be realized in full.

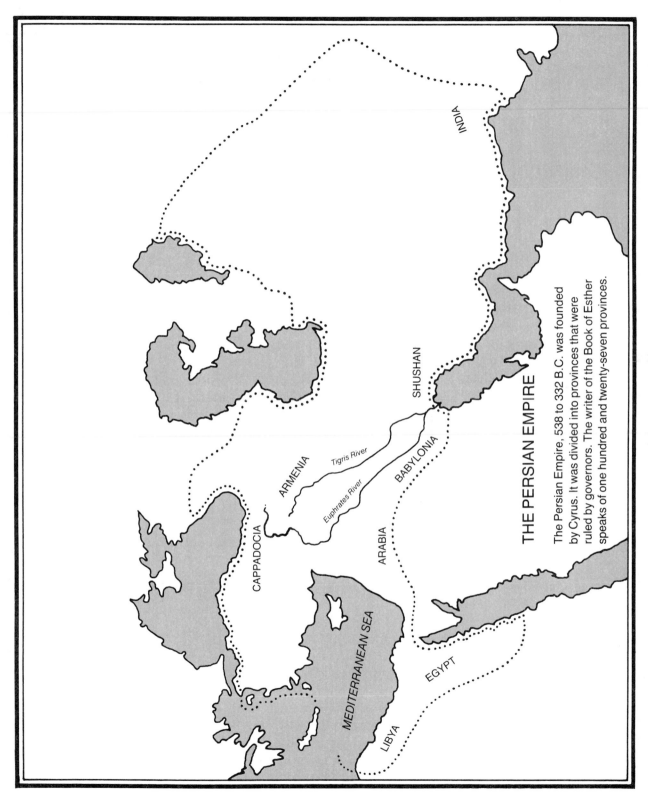

THE PERSIAN EMPIRE

The Persian Empire, 538 to 332 B.C. was founded by Cyrus. It was divided into provinces that were ruled by governors. The writer of the Book of Esther speaks of one hundred and twenty-seven provinces.

INDIA

SHUSHAN

ARMENIA

Tigris River

Euphrates River

BABYLONIA

ARABIA

CAPPADOCIA

MEDITERRANEAN SEA

EGYPT

LIBYA

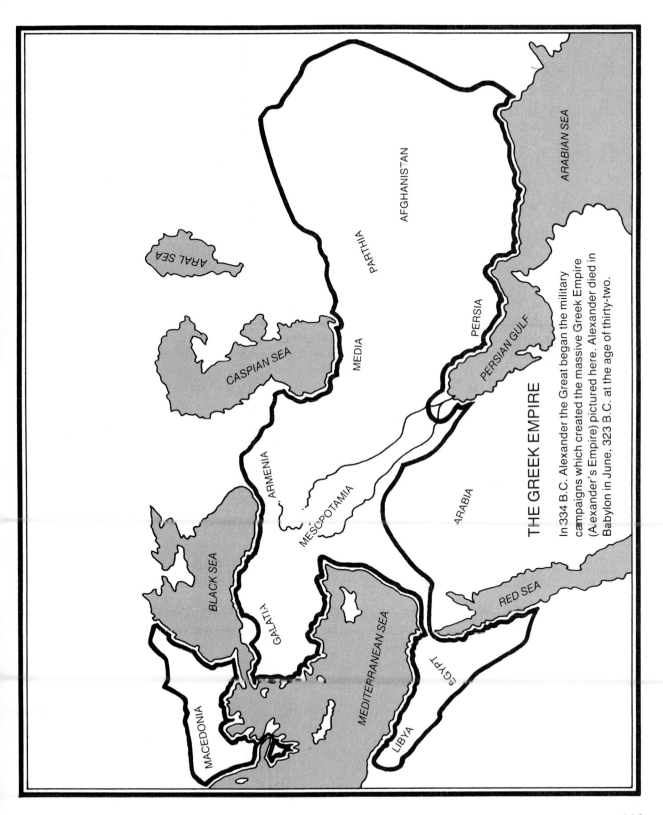

THE GREEK EMPIRE

In 334 B.C. Alexander the Great began the military campaigns which created the massive Greek Empire (Alexander's Empire) pictured here. Alexander died in Babylon in June, 323 B.C. at the age of thirty-two.

ARABIAN SEA

AFGHANISTAN

PARTHIA

PERSIA

PERSIAN GULF

ARAL SEA

CASPIAN SEA

MEDIA

ARMENIA

MESOPOTAMIA

ARABIA

RED SEA

BLACK SEA

GALATIA

MEDITERRANEAN SEA

EGYPT

MACEDONIA

LIBYA

By the time of Jesus, Rome had replaced Greece as the dominant power in the world. The early Christians were quite right theologically to substitute Rome for Greece in interpreting Daniel's statue-vision. But the point was made for then and for all the centuries that have followed—any "might-is-right" secular state that oppresses the people of God is doomed to be destroyed by the supernatural "stone." Every nation in all of time is subject to the judgment of God from Nebuchadnezzar to Antiochus IV to the Caesars to the tyrants of all passing centuries, including the Hitlers and the Stalins. The Roman emperor Julian the Apostate (332–363 A.D.), persecutor of Christians, on his deathbed admitted defeat and said, "Galilean, you have won."

The writer of the Book of Daniel warmed the hearts of his readers when he wrote of the haughty Nebuchadnezzar falling down before Daniel in homage (2:46). Daniel and his friends received promotions and presents and Daniel remained at the king's court (2:47–49). This second wisdom story, then, teaches that human wisdom is feeble compared to that given by God. It also teaches that God controls the destinies of nations and that one day He will establish an everlasting kingdom. Further, it assures the believers in dire peril that God has not forgotten nor forsaken them; God will give them strength for today and hope for tomorrow.

A Wisdom Story of Daniel's Three Friends: How Martyrdom is Preferable to Apostasy (3:1–30)
The Colossal Golden Image and the King's Law

This part of our Scripture lesson contains a typical "martyr story," powerful and moving, of how God rescues and delivers His faithful followers.

We read that Nebuchadnezzar set up a huge idol—ninety by nine feet—of his favorite god on the plain of Dura in the province of Babylon. There the king assembled his official family—satraps, prefects, governors, counselors, treasurers, justices, and magistrates—to witness its dedication. And he then gave the order that everyone was to bow down to the image when the proper musical sound was given. Failure to worship at the prescribed time meant execution, so most of the conforming citizens no doubt found it easy to follow the order out of their fear of the fiery furnace (3:1–7).

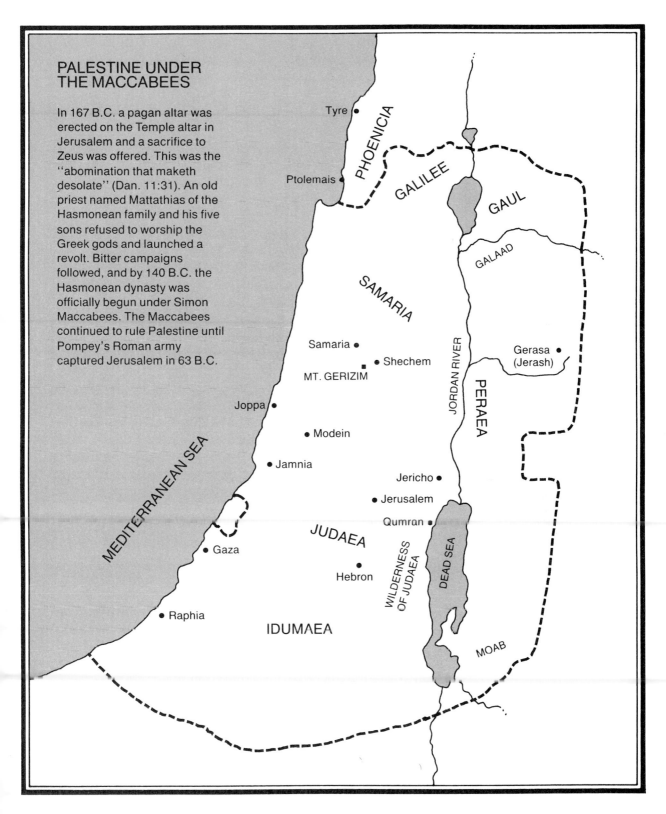

PALESTINE UNDER THE MACCABEES

In 167 B.C. a pagan altar was erected on the Temple altar in Jerusalem and a sacrifice to Zeus was offered. This was the "abomination that maketh desolate" (Dan. 11:31). An old priest named Mattathias of the Hasmonean family and his five sons refused to worship the Greek gods and launched a revolt. Bitter campaigns followed, and by 140 B.C. the Hasmonean dynasty was officially begun under Simon Maccabees. The Maccabees continued to rule Palestine until Pompey's Roman army captured Jerusalem in 63 B.C.

Tyre

PHOENICIA

GALILEE

GAUL

Ptolemais

GALAAD

SAMARIA

JORDAN RIVER

PERAEA

Samaria

Shechem

Gerasa
(Jerash)

MT. GERIZIM

MEDITERRANEAN SEA

Joppa

Modein

Jamnia

Jericho

Jerusalem

Qumran

JUDAEA

Gaza

WILDERNESS OF JUDAEA

DEAD SEA

Hebron

Raphia

IDUMΛEA

MOAB

131

The author of Daniel wrote the story in majestic, stilted, sonorous tones, but it gives every indication of a bit of tongue-in-cheek writing. He was using this literary device to poke sarcastic fun at idol worship—the idol may be awe inspiring in its size but it was still only a dumb idol. The author's jibe is that the idol is a pygmy in contrast to the awesome greatness of God. He may have intended his readers to see in Nebuchadnezzar a likeness to Antiochus IV who had set up an altar to Zeus in the Temple in Jerusalem, demanding that the Jews worship Greek gods on pain of death. The plea in this story—to remain loyal to God in the face of persecution—was meaningful to them even as it is to modern Christians in certain Third World countries.

In the days of the early church the Christians were forced to worship the emperor Caesar on threat of banishment or death. The all-powerful claims of some totalitarian states in the twentieth century are little different from emperor worship. There must be a limit to the demands that any state can make. A state or an institution can expect the loyalty and sacrifice of its people, but it cannot coerce worship and love. John Calvin, the Protestant reformer, said that when the prince obeys God, the Christian should obey the prince. But when the prince disobeys God, the Christian has a right to remove the prince from office.

The Refusal to Conform

Next, as we move ahead in our story, the drama is intensified (3:8–12). Shadrach, Meshach, and Abednego refused to worship the image and were reported to the authorities by malicious colleagues. A totalitarian state always creates informers because it cannot operate without them. The story of how Anne Frank and her family were betrayed by informers to the German Gestapo during the Second World War still tugs at our hearts and consciences. In her *Diary,* Anne recorded how the Jewish Frank family was forced to hide from the Nazi authorities in a factory attic in Amsterdam for two long years. Young Anne's spirit gave them courage to go on when they lost all hope. Their saga could be the story of any group of human beings forced to live in fear, while giving way to irritations caused by constricted conditions. Finally, the Franks were turned in by informers, and all but the father died in concentration camps. Then, and now, there is something in our spirit that reacts in revulsion to a totalitarian state and the informers that keep it in power.

The three young Jews were apprehended and hauled before Nebuchadnezzar and asked if they had indeed refused to bow down before the statue as ordered (3:13–18). The king was in a furious rage, but before the three could answer he gave them another chance to fulfill the requirement and escape death. But Shadrach, Meshach, and Abednego gave a dramatic but quick and confident answer, "O Nebuchadnezzar, we are not careful to answer thee [we don't really need to answer you] in this matter. If it be so, our God whom we serve is able to deliver us from the burning fiery furance, and he will deliver us out of thine hand, O king. But if not, be it known unto thee, O king, that we will not serve thy gods, nor worship the golden image which thou hast set up" (3:17–18). Even though they acknowledged in these words the possibility that God might withhold His aid, yet they refused to compromise their faith in Him. Yes, they had a strong desire to live, but, if necessary, they were ready to die. For the author of the Book of Daniel, "meaning," not "escape" was the product of faith in God. To have bowed before Nebuchadnezzar's idol would have destroyed the very meaning that made life worth living.

The 1981 British movie *Chariots of Fire* gave us the story of a young Scot who was the son of missionaries in China and a young Jew whose father was an immigrant from Lithuania. Both of these young men were runners of considerable skill. One of the sharpest moments in the film came at the 1924 Olympics when the young Scot, Eric Liddell, was asked by the foppish Prince of Wales to run and compete on the Sabbath. Liddell explained patiently to the prince why he would not violate his conscience by going against what he believed. The scene ended with Liddell looking far more princely than the Prince of Wales. But the young Scot went on to achieve deserved glory. Although years later Eric Liddell died in a Japanese concentration camp in China during the Second World War, the memory of his defiance of consequences still serves as a good model. In a similar way the bravery of those three young Jews in the face of Nebuchadnezzar's threat has inspired God's people in all time who refused to worship idols of any kind.

Mockery and Miracle

When King Nebuchadnezzar heard the refusal of the three young Jews, he flew into a rage. I have to believe that the Daniel writer deliberately inserted mockery into the tone of the story as he described the exaggerated rage of the king. The detail here is delightful (3:19–23) as we're told that the furnace was fired up seven times hotter than usual. Then the king instructed his mightiest men to throw the three Jews into the inferno—fully dressed, including their hats. The king's instructions were carried out, but the furnace was so hot that the execution detail were burned to a crisp.

Now, though, the story assumes a unique and marvelous twist (3:24–30). When Nebuchadnezzar peered into the furnace, he saw four, not three, men, unaffected by the flames. In amazement he said to his counsellors, "Lo, I see four men loose, walking in the midst of the fire, and they have no hurt; and the form of the fourth is like the Son of God." Then, right in front of everybody the king asked the men to come out of the furnace.

Note the scene described by the writer, "And the princes, governors, and captains, and the king's counsellors, being gathered together, saw these men, upon whose bodies the fire had no power, *nor was an hair of their head singed, neither were their coats changed, nor the smell of fire had passed on them*" (3:27, italics mine). In his attempt to defy God, Nebuchadnezzar ended up looking very foolish. But then we see that at least he had the good sense to recognize the greatness of the Hebrews' God, and "the king promoted Shadrach, Meshach, and Abednego, in the province of Babylon."

The message was clear to the first readers of the Book of Daniel and to God's people of every century. No king or ruler can resist the power of God, for He is in control of history. And we can be confident of the truth that while we may experience our fiery furnaces of difficulty and hard times, we don't have to confront them alone.

Then, too, there may be those times when it seems as if all of the forces of evil are in the world's driver's seat. But the people of God, we twentieth-century Christians, can know without question that our Creator-God is in control of His universe. Our hope is in Him, and we can look ahead to that day when everyone and everything will "confess that Jesus Christ is Lord, to the glory of God the Father" (Phil. 2:11).

Many Bible interpreters have rightly called the Book of Daniel a tract of encouragement—a book of hope, and it is that. On May 23, 1939 the submarine *Squalus* sank off of Portsmouth, New Hampshire. When the rescue squad reached the submerged vessel, they tapped on the metal hull a question in Morse code. The trapped men inside the sub tapped back, "Is there any hope?" And there was, for the McCann rescue bell was used successfully for the first time as thirty-three surviving men were saved.

The message of the Book of Daniel is electrifying: There is hope for God's people; we are never alone!

Father God, Thank You for the hedge of protection You've placed around me—when I pass through the fire, even my hair is not singed! You have fully enveloped me in Your love. AMEN.

WHAT THIS SCRIPTURE MEANS TO ME
Daniel 1—3

Several years ago I entered graduate school to obtain a master's degree in theology. Because I was still single at that time, I lived in the women's dormitory on campus. There were several advantages to living in the dormitory community. I enjoyed the close fellowship with other on-campus students. I didn't have to buck the rush-hour traffic on my way to early morning classes. And all of my meals were provided, which meant that more time could be devoted to studying rather than grocery shopping and cooking.

A few days after the first semester began, I overheard a rather heated discussion at the dinner table. Two students in particular sounded extremely dissatisfied with the quality and variety of food which were available in the cafeteria. My initial reaction was one of great surprise and disbelief. I had been quite impressed with the meals which had been served. The portions were more than adequate, and I thought that most of the food tasted fairly close to "good-ole-home-cookin'." I began to feel annoyed by these complaints which seemed unfair to and overly critical of the kitchen staff.

After listening to this conversation for a few moments, I gradually realized that the students who were the most upset were more irritated with the college administrators than with the cooks. I was surprised to learn that they were strict vegetarians. They had to pay for food which they couldn't eat. They had been denied permission to supplement the meat dishes with additional vegetables. And they were not allowed to prepare their own meals in their dormitory rooms. They felt they were being discriminated against and misunderstood. They were angry because the administration refused to consider any changes in the standard meal plan. And they were extremely annoyed because their commitment to a strict vegetarian diet was not being respected.

This incident came to mind immediately as I read the first chapter of Daniel. Verses 8 through 16 state the dilemma which Daniel faced, and his determination not to "defile himself with the king's rich food, or with the wine which he drank" (1:8). Daniel and his friends, like the students in graduate school, had to defend their commitment to a diet which others considered unusual, even eccentric.

For me, there are two lessons to be learned from this passage. The first deals with the issues of respect and tolerance. I think I need to develop greater tolerance and understanding for people whose life-styles, habits, or patterns of behavior differ from mine. I pray for the ability to respect, be considerate of, and accept people for *who* they are rather than for *what* they do.

Second, I believe this incident in Daniel's life contains a message for all people. I am writing this segment during our annual parish stewardship campaign. For several weeks now, sermons have focused on each Christian's responsibility to be a good steward—of time, talents, treasure, creation, and relationships. In an indirect way, I think Daniel is urging us to be good stewards of ourselves—our bodies and our health. His hymn of thanksgiving (cf. 2:20–23) praises God for His gifts of wisdom, knowledge, understanding, and strength, reflecting his belief that all that we are—in mind and body—is a gift from God, and should be cared for in the best way possible.

LESSON 6
Daniel 4–6

Faith in God: Its Deliverance of the Faithful

Father God, I know that if I follow You wholeheartedly and trust You, I'll be able to conquer the giants in my life. AMEN.

A Wisdom Story of Nebuchadnezzar's Second Dream: A Monarch Who Tries to Rule Apart From God or Against God is Mad (4:1–37)

The story in this section was written to show that the pride of great rulers—be they Nebuchadnezzar or Antiochus or Hitler—is a form of madness that brings its own judgment. God will see to it that haughty kings and kingdoms are brought low through their faulty faith. By contrast, the right kind of faith in the true God always brings sanity to world rulers. And the goodness of God will give even dumb leaders the hope of a new beginning.

Nebuchadnezzar's Dream of a Giant Tree

Our story starts out now with Nebuchadnezzar sending a letter or decree to all his subjects. He pictured himself as a world ruler who wanted only peace and harmony for his people. In verse form he praised the God of Israel for all the good things that had been given to him and he acknowledged the greatness of God and His everlasting kingdom and rule (4:1–3).

After explaining how he had come to appreciate the God of Daniel, he told about a dream that had alarmed him (4:4–18). Unlike his earlier dream, he remembered the details of this second dream. As he had done previously, he called on all the wise men who were expected to help him interpret the dream. But none of them were able to give him any interpretation. Finally, Daniel appeared on the scene to interpret the haunting dream.

The king recognized in Daniel "the spirit of the holy gods" because by that time Daniel's reputation for wisdom and interpretation was well known. Here again the author of Daniel mirrors the story of Joseph in Egypt (Gen. 41:38) and his ability to interpret Pharaoh's dream. The focal point of Nebuchadnezzar's graphic dream was a giant tree that reached up to heaven, was visible to the whole earth, that provided food for everybody, and was a shelter for birds and animals. In the dream a heavenly messenger had the tree cut down to a stump, and even the stump was bound with a band of brass and iron. The person that the tree represented had to share the lot of the helpless animals until he learned that God was the real ruler of the universe. Furthermore, this unknown person was to be as dumb as a beast for seven years until he learned this lesson.

Three familiar symbols were at work in this dream-story. First, the ancient world often spoke of the rule of a king as a spreading tree. Ezekiel had already compared the rule of Pharaoh to a great cedar (Ezek. 31) that fell through its grandiose delusions. Second, the "watchers" or "holy ones" were common figures in apocalyptic literature. They were a class of supernatural beings who sat in God's heavenly council, took orders from Him, carried out His commands, and interceded for the humans on the earth. Third, the Old Testament prophets had long taught that God humbled the proud and lifted up the humble. The seventh theme of the prophets was that the voice of authority was most likely not the voice of God because the power of rulers tended to become abusive. For example, rulers like Nebuchadnezzar and Antiochus forgot that they were creatures and not the Creator. They refused to acknowledge that God was in control of His world.

When Nebuchadnezzar had finished telling Daniel the content of his dream, he then said, "Now thou, O Belteshazzar [Daniel's Babylonian name], declare

Daniel's Interpretation of the Dream

the interpretation thereof, forasmuch as all the wise men of my kingdom are not able to make known unto me the interpretation: but thou art able; for the spirit of the holy gods is in thee" (4:18).

As Daniel had listened to the dream, our writer says that he "was astonied for one hour, and his thoughts troubled him [Daniel was amazed and troubled]" (4:19). Daniel had hoped that the king's dream was about his enemies, but unfortunately, it was about the king himself (4:20–27).

Daniel saw that Nebuchadnezzar was the cut down tree. He further saw that the king, because of his arrogance and pride, would be insane and eat grass like an ox for a period of seven years. But then Daniel saw the element of hope in the dream—there was hope for Nebuchadnezzar because the "stump" of the tree and its roots were intact. This meant that when the king learned his lesson and recognized the sovereignty of God, he could be restored, even as the tree could grow again from its stump and roots (4:26).

Then with God-given boldness Daniel completed his interpretation by saying, "Wherefore, O king, let my counsel be acceptable unto thee, and break off thy sins by righteousness [stop sinning and do what is right], and thine iniquities by shewing mercy to the poor; if it may be a lengthening of thy tranquility [then your mind will be at peace]" (4:27).

In other words, the king could get his act together again by repenting to God and having a right attitude toward his people—if he learned from his mistakes and the beating he had gotten from life, he would be a better king. Norman Rockwell, the famous American artist and illustrator, once said, "When I want a dog model, I always get it from the pound. Dogs that have taken a beating from life have character."

The Dream Fulfilled

Next, we're told that a year passed by with nothing happening. But then we see and hear Nebuchadnezzar as he strolls complacently back and forth in his palace, "Is not this great Babylon, *that I have built* for the house of the kingdom *by the might of my power, and for the honour of my majesty?"* (4:30, italics mine). As Nebuchadnezzar looked out across the magnificence of his city and country, he swelled up with pride at "what I have built." Bertrand Russell could have been speaking about both Nebuchadnezzar and Antiochus IV when he noted that all of us would like to be God if possible, and some few find it difficult to admit the impossibility.

The archaeological findings in Babylon's ruins most certainly point to the grandeur of Nebuchadnezzar's efforts. But it wasn't the grandeur of his accomplishments that brought on his downfall ultimately—it was his pride and arrogance.

In response to the king's boastfulness "there fell a voice from heaven, saying, O king Nebuchadnezzar, to thee it is spoken; The kingdom is departed from thee." And the voice added the sentence that for seven years he would be insane and would live like an animal (4:31–32).

Pride and lack of thanks usually go hand in hand, and I know that I'm usually most stuck on myself when I'm least grateful to God for what He has given me. On the old Garry Moore show, *To Tell the Truth,* Moore interviewed three heroic high school boys about their daring feat of rescue. The three had been standing on a subway platform in New York City when suddenly a man fell on the tracks below. Instantly and without thinking the boys jumped to the tracks and snatched the man from in front of an approaching train. They received citations of bravery from the mayor and several organizations. When Garry Moore asked them if they had heard from the rescued man or his family, one of the boys said, "No, he never thanked us." King Nebuchadnezzar never returned to give thanks, either, for all that God had given him. Few things are as unkind as ingratitude, while nothing is more fitting to the Christian than gratitude.

The Daniel writer followed the Old Testament prophets in his estimation that pride was at the bottom of all the great mistakes of the ruling class or the kingly families. Queen Elizabeth I of England (1533–1603) fits this pattern, and her pride caused her much suffering. Her favorite courtier was the Earl of Essex who, caught in a plot, was sentenced to die. Elizabeth was eager to pardon him because she really loved him, but she said, "I will save him, but only if he humbles himself and asks me to." When she didn't hear from Essex, he was executed. Elizabeth was heartbroken and her health began to fail. A long time later one of her ladies-in-waiting lay dying and called for the queen. She confessed to Elizabeth that Essex had given her a letter pleading for his life, but since she hated Essex and wanted him executed, she had withheld the message. Elizabeth was so crushed by this confession that she never recovered and spent her last days mourning for Essex. Her pride was her undoing and nearly drove her insane.

The King's Sanity Restored

Nebuchadnezzar's ultimate insanity was to think he was God, and in failing to recognize God's rule, he lost his own. When the king got his faith back in the right perspective, he got his kingdom back. In humility the king said, when I "lifted up mine eyes unto heaven . . . mine understanding returned unto me" (4:34). The "stump" grew back into a big tree even greater than before. Nebuchadnezzar's pride led him to madness, but his simple trust in God led him back to sanity. By the grace of God the king got a second chance. How thankful we can be for a God of the second chance!

A Wisdom Story of Belshazzar's Feast (5:1–31)

The scene shifts now to the grandson of Nebuchadnezzar, Belshazzar, who is now king. It is readily apparent that Belshazzar had not learned from his predecessors. And added to his arrogance and pride was the sin of using the sacred vessels taken from the Jerusalem Temple at his banquet-orgy. Nebuchadnezzar had learned humility the hard way through his years of insanity. Now, as we will see, Belshazzar refused to learn the lesson and perished. Antiochus IV in 165 B.C. had yet to learn the lesson, but he would soon.

In this part of our Scripture lesson the author of the Book of Daniel focused on three things. First, we shall see as the story unfolds, Belshazzar made a fool of himself by his insolent and flippant behavior. Second, Belshazzar had committed the terrible act of sacrilege by profaning the Temple vessels. Third, God was on the side of the enslaved and beleaguered Jews. The first readers of the Book of Daniel would see the parallels with the actions of Antiochus IV. The Jews might appear to be defeated, but God was still in control.

The drunken banquet described here (5:1–4) was a common event among royalty in the ancient world. Belshazzar threw a wild party for hundreds of his top lords and ladies at which he committed the ultimate blasphemy against God. His predecessor Nebuchadnezzar had been arrogant, but he became insolent and sacrilegious, high-handedly passing judgment on God Himself.

Belshazzar's Banquet

During the drinking and revelry Belshazzar moved beyond merriment to malice—he ordered the gold and silver goblets and basins of the Jerusalem Temple to be brought out. He gave these sacred vessels to his guests to use as wine cups while they praised their own idols of gold, silver, bronze, iron, wood, and stone. Belshazzar, then, deliberately profaned holy objects and publicly declared that the God of the captured Jews could be mocked with impunity. He arrogated to himself the right to mock God's majesty and laugh at His authority. This scene of heavy-footed treading on the sacred would have struck the original readers of Daniel with special poignancy because Antiochus IV was doing the very same thing to God's sacred Temple objects in their day. But in the next verses the original readers were to see that Belshazzar's judgment was quick and devastating, and were encouraged to believe that Antiochus's end would be just as swift and sure.

During the drunken sacrilege there suddenly appeared a single ghostly hand which began to write on the plaster of the wall (5:5–9). The king's nerve snapped, and his haughtiness turned to terror—his face blanched, his arms grew weak, and his knees knocked together. The quaking king immediately sent for the wise men to get into the room, read the writing, and tell him its meaning.

The Writing on the Wall

Instead of threatening to tear the wise men limb from limb if they could not clear up the puzzle as Nebuchadnezzar had done, Belshazzar promised them money and promotions. But the professional wise men could not crack the riddle. Instead, only Daniel, because of his God-given insight and inspiration, was equal to the task. The author of Daniel was being deliberately satirical at this point as he wanted his readers to see that in a land famous for its wise men, only Daniel the Jew was truly wise.

Daniel's Lecture

We next learn that the queen, a woman of obvious power and influence, arrived on the scene and encouraged the king not to be overly distressed. She reminded him that Daniel, a wise man appointed by Nebuchadnezzar, could unravel the puzzle of the handwriting on the wall, "now let Daniel be called, and he will shew the interpretation" (5:12). She made it clear that she had confidence in Daniel for three reasons: He could interpret dreams (Chapters 2 & 4); he could make the obscure plain; and he was gifted in solving knotty problems like the mysterious handwriting on the wall.

In response to the queen's suggestion, Belshazzar summoned Daniel and promised him a rich reward for interpreting the writing on the wall (5:13–16). In a few clipped sentences Daniel made it clear that he had no interest in rewards. Then he proceeded to deliver a two point lecture to the king and everyone assembled in the banquet room. In this lecture Daniel stated that God had made Nebuchadnezzar and the kingdom of Babylon great, but because the king had acted as if he were God, he had suffered dire humiliation until he came to himself. Second, Belshazzar had refused to learn from his grandfather's mistakes, and because of his own pride and idolatry God had placed a message in mysterious handwriting on the banquet room wall.

We can't help but be startled at Daniel's boldness before the Babylonian dictator, and his scorn of consequences; but then we remember the three things that Jesus told His disciples in the Sermon on the Mount (Matt. 5–7): They would be fearless, they would be joyful, and they would be in trouble. The disciples did get into trouble, and discovered that they were unafraid. They joyfully laughed at their own troubles, and only cried over the troubles of others.

After delivering this biting lecture to Belshazzar, Daniel read and interpreted the message. The writing was MENE, MENE, TEKEL, UPHARSIN. Today we would read it as: "Counted; a mina (a weight or coin), a shekel (one sixtieth of a mina), and a couple or half minas." This may have been a common Babylonian jingle about weights (or coins), but Daniel gave these words a divine interpretation that pronounced doom upon the king. He turned a jingle into God's judgment.

Both the Hebrew and the Aramaic languages were able to change the meaning of words by changing their sounds. From this we get the interpretation, "Your days are numbered and time has run out. You have been weighed in the balances and have failed the test. Your kingdom will be divided and given to the Medes and Persians."

To the Jews suffering under Antiochus IV this must have been a parable of comfort and encouragement. The author of Daniel consistently drove home the lesson that all eminent leaders are under the judgment of God who alone gives or rescinds their authority. God used madness to bring Nebuchadnezzar to sane humility; Belshazzar persisted in his pride and was brought low; the mad egotism of Antiochus IV was about to catch up with him in a final retribution. No leader can flout God's will and expect to get away with it. Sir Winston Churchill, speaking of Hitler and Mussolini in 1936, said, "Dictators ride to and fro upon tigers which they dare not dismount. And the tigers are getting hungry."

At first Daniel had turned down the king's promised reward, saying, "Let thy gifts be to thyself, and give thy rewards to another." Daniel didn't want to be indebted to the monarch because he knew he had to say some tough things to the king. But Belshazzar overrode Daniel's protest and gave him a high place of honor in the kingdom. Belshazzar also overrode Daniel's blistering lecture and made no move to repent of his pride. And finally we read, "In that night" Belshazzar was overtaken by judgment and he was

The Interpretation of the Mysterious Message

A Wise Man's Reward and a Foolish King's Punishment

Pictured here amongst the Babylonian ruins are bricks said to have been made by the Jewish captives during the time of the Exile. These were shaped and made with mud and straw.

"slain" (5:29). This was meant by the author of Daniel to serve as a warning to Antiochus IV, and to any other earthly ruler, that a challenge to God's authority carries its own judgment.

In a page out of American history we read that the battle of King's Mountain, fought on October 7, 1780, put an end to the proud boast of the British Major Patrick Ferguson that "neither God Almighty nor all the rebels in hell could drive him off the hilltop." Ferguson had been threatening the colonials in the Carolinas and Tennessee to put them to death and burn their whole country if they didn't take the oath of allegiance to the British Crown. Far from being cowed by Ferguson's threats, the rebellious pioneer riflemen of the frontier settlements resolved to teach the British major humility. Ferguson's pride, determination to chastise, and hunger for glory brought about his disaster at King's Mountain, the "turning point of the Revolution in the South." Toward the end of the battle, Major Ferguson was blasted from his saddle by a volley of rifle fire, and his riddled body was buried by the Whig militia at the foot of the hill.

As a boy I used to picnic with my family at the battle ground and play "soldier" around Ferguson's grave. The battle was fought near the corner of the land owned by my great-great-great grandfather, Arthur Patterson, Sr., and he was one of the American soldiers killed in the battle. His name is on the tall marble Federal Monument that towers over the field today. That cruel, rainy, unseasonably chilly Saturday afternoon of over two centuries ago haunted my childhood with the lesson that "Proud men propose, but God disposes." The Book of Daniel teaches that pride is an affront to God, and the best laid plans of the haughty are always under His judgment.

In verse 31 we read that "Darius the Median took the kingdom, being about threescore and two years old." History gives us no record of a Median dynasty between the Babylonian and Persian. We do know that Cyrus the Great of Persia conquered Babylon in 539 B.C. and became its king. The author of the Book of Daniel was not trying to be a modern historian with computer accuracy, but a theologian telling past stories to drive home the point that God is the Lord of history and He will be with His people in their time of pain to see them through.

A Wisdom Story of Daniel in the Lion's Den: God Will Deliver His Faithful Servants (6:1–28)

The story of Daniel in the lion's den is one of the best known stories in the Bible—a story of jealousy, intrigue, and threatened death in which God rescued His faithful follower and destroyed the betrayers. The storyteller of the Book of Daniel reached back into the Persian period for this event and adapted it to the needs of his own day to reassure his readers of ultimate victory against Antiochus IV. If Daniel could not compromise those religious principles which he held dear, then neither could they.

This story is told in part to give us courage. But courage is such a strange thing: On some days I have it, but on other days I have about as much courage as a mouse. Daniel serves us as a model of how to prepare years ahead of time to be brave when the test finally comes. I hope someday to be like a certain lame man who came to join the army. The other soldiers laughed at him and said, "How can you run with that lame leg?" To which the lame man replied, "I came to fight, not to run."

I must confess that my faith in Christ has not cost me the kind of suffering experienced by Daniel and his three friends. I have never starved for food nor been locked in jail. No one has ever thrown a stone at me because of my faith. I haven't been persecuted, and I enjoy a religious freedom that was won for me by my forefathers. They died that I might worship God in peace. I have studied their lives, and I know how they suffered, but as for me I have benefitted from Christ's death rather than shared in His pain. I bow in humble gratitude, then, before Daniel and all the numberless others who went through torment that I might enjoy a religious freedom that they never knew.

Daniel's Jealous Associates

Under Nebuchadnezzar Daniel's services were so outstanding that he had become chief of the "wise men"; under Belshazzar he had become the third ruler of the empire; under Darius he was about to be appointed Prime Minister of the kingdom (6:1–3). Like his three friends, Shadrach, Meshach, and

Abednego, he had to endure a terrible trial rather than betray his faith in God. His three friends had been commanded by the king to worship an idol, but he was commanded not to worship any god but the king.

The other bureaucrats in the Persian system apparently felt threatened by Daniel's new powers, but could find no fault in his public conduct of his office. These jealous and vindictive office holders then began to spy on his private life to find some grounds of complaint. They said, "We shall not find any occasion against this Daniel, except we find it against him concerning the law of his God" (6:5). They snooped where his convictions were strongest—in his private devotional habits to his God.

If the measure of our character is what we do when we think no one is looking, then Daniel's character was found out while he was at prayer. They caught him praying without state sanction and hatched a plot against him. Daniel had stepped out of line, and they thought they had him. It was suddenly too dangerous for Daniel to be right in matters on which the established authorities were wrong.

The jealous plotters cleverly suggested to the king "that whosoever shall ask a petition of any God or man for thirty days, save of thee, O king, he shall be cast into the den of lions" (6:7). Such a loyalty oath was common in the ancient Middle East, and the king signed it into law without a second thought. Antiochus IV had resorted to the same kind of arrogant self-deification, so the original readers of the book would have readily associated with Daniel and the trap that had been set for him.

The Law Versus Conscience

When Daniel heard about the new laws, he did what came naturally for him, "he went into his house; and his windows being open in his chamber toward Jerusalem, he kneeled upon his knees three times a day, and prayed, and gave thanks before his God, as he did aforetime" (6:10). What Daniel did might have momentarily been illegal, but it was not immoral. Sometimes we need to obey the state (Rom. 13); sometimes we need to disobey the state

(Rev. 13); and to distinguish between the two takes the wisdom of a Daniel. When the state demands the loyalty that belongs to God, then the state comes under the judgment of God.

But what about this matter of striving for coercive power for me as a Christian? Didn't Jesus' servant way of life set for me a model of humility—the willingness to endure obscurity, misunderstanding, and shame? When I desire and strive for visible prestige through coercive power, don't I enter into a major dimension of sin that the prophets talked about? Indeed I do! But what if I never have the chance to get my hands on the levers of power, become an eminent person of prestige, and join the oppressor class? Most of us will never even get close to that temptation because we are among the oppressed. But I still want security, so don't I quietly cuddle up to those in power in order to gain their favor, keep my job, and enjoy their protection? Indeed I do, and this is the other major dimension of sin that the prophets talked about—the sin of passivity. My inordinate longing for security under the wing of the powerful often makes me passive and fearful about the risks involved in changing a situation of social injustice or changing myself.

Evil flourishes when good people are passive; truth can be outraged by silence. My worldly striving for prestige, power, and security becomes sinful when it leads me to swear allegiance to institutions, ideologies, attitudes, or persons which conflict with Jesus' servantlike way of total dependence on God. Daniel, a man of power, gives to us—mostly people without power—a model to imitate. He didn't cringe before the threat of a despot; and, he didn't grovel in the face of coercive power to retain his security. Daniel, like Jesus, looked at death, the final threat that power holds over us, and did not flinch.

When the conspirators presented Darius with evidence of Daniel's disobedience, the king realized he had been maneuvered into an impossible position. He tried to get Daniel out of the trap, but the plotters reminded him of his solemn pledge. Darius saw through the conspiracy but was helpless, and he reluctantly "commanded, and they brought Daniel, and cast him into the den of lions" (6:16). Like Jesus in the garden of Gethsemane, Daniel went to his doom. He was dropped into the lion's pit with the words of the king ringing in his ears, "Daniel, thy God whom thou servest continually, he will deliver thee" (6:16).

Daniel's Deliverance

This next scene (6:18–24) would have been especially encouraging to those original readers of the Book of Daniel. If God had brought Daniel to power in the past and protected him from death, surely God would do the same for them in the present if they remained loyal in their prayers. Just as loyalty to God was Daniel's best defense under Darius, so loyalty to God would be their best defense under Antiochus IV.

We next learn that Darius spent the night wide awake and fasting (6:18), worrying whether or not Daniel's God had rescued him. Early the next morning he hurried to the pit and called down anxiously, "O Daniel, servant of the living God, is thy God, whom thou servest continually, able to deliver thee from the lions?" (6:20). With relief and joy he heard Daniel call back, "My God hath sent his angel, and hath shut the lions' mouths, that they have not hurt me" (6:22). Daniel was immediately hauled out of the pit without a scratch on him. Like his three friends in the fiery furnace, he emerged without any sign of his ordeal.

The author's lessons here for his readers are the same as they were for Shadrach, Meshach, and Abednego under Nebuchadnezzar. Faith in God may get us into trouble, but that same faith will see us through the trouble. God will countermand human laws to rescue His faithful ones, so we have every right to believe in God's saving power (Heb. 11; 1 Peter 5:8; 2 Cor. 1:8 ff.). Daniel's righteousness was his best defense, but what about those of us today who don't have his unblemished track record? Will God protect those of us who have fouled our nest? We learn from Jesus Christ that there are none of us who are perfect, but that our loving heavenly Father redeems the less than perfect who have faith. It's up to us to believe without question that God has accepted us just as we are, blemishes and all.

The author of the Book of Daniel, to further drive home the lesson to his readers that the faithful flourish while the evil perish, tells of the horrible end of Daniel's enemies (6:24). If hell is defined as "truth seen too late," then they were too late. They tripped over their own viciousness and ended up in the pit. They showed their own character by the way they vilified Daniel's character. God had shut the mouths of the lions for Daniel, but He left them open for his conspirators, and they were eaten. The plotters and their families suffered the fate that they had planned for Daniel.

Darius's Faith in Daniel's God

The author of Daniel wanted his readers to get one more theological lesson from the lion's den story. He wanted them to see that the God they served created and deposed world empires, but His kingdom would last forever. Darius confessed his faith in Daniel's God and put it in the form of a decree to the whole world. First, Darius said that the God of the Jews was a "living God," always active on behalf of His people. Second, He was a stable God whose sovereignty was constant always, "even unto the end." And third, He was a God who "delivereth and rescueth" His faithful ones even from "the power of the lions," and caused Daniel to prosper into the reign of Cyrus the Persian. The Babylonians and Medes did not convert to the Jewish faith historically, but the "lion's den" story is a wonderful confession of faith in God.

And just as these six wonderful wisdom stories gave comfort and assurance to the persecuted people of God in the second century B.C., they can also comfort us with the promise that God is with us in our troubles. Times have changed, but God has not changed nor has pain changed. We can relax because God is with us as He was with Daniel and his three friends in exile. William Quale, the Methodist bishop of Kansas in the nineteenth century, in the midst of a restless night suddenly awoke at 4 A.M. He heard a great voice saying, "William, this is God. You may go to sleep now. I am awake." And that same divine voice has come down through all those centuries since the time of Daniel saying, "I am awake. You may go to sleep now." He is still the God of all comfort, and our hearts are not as restless as they were.

God, You are a living God, always active on behalf of Your people; You deliver and rescue even from the power of lions—I can rest in Your goodness. AMEN.

WHAT THIS SCRIPTURE MEANS TO ME
Daniel 4—6

In 1969 I learned an important and life-changing lesson about personal relationships. I had been dating the same young man for several years. We participated in all the important high school functions together—football and basketball games, Junior-Senior proms, class plays, fund raisers, and special events. During our final two years in high school, we were virtually inseparable.

During the summer months, also, we spent a lot of time together—playing tennis, having picnics in roadside parks, visiting each other's relatives, and having long talks about our hopes and dreams for the future. The subject of marriage never came up during those early years as our relationship grew, but I did think to myself on several occasions, "I bet we'll get married some day. We like so many of the same things. We have the same goals and aspirations. Our life-styles are quite similar. We like each other's families. And we hardly ever argue or disagree about anything."

We approached our high school graduation with mixed feelings. Along with our classmates, we experienced the excitement and sense of accomplishment and pride resulting from four years of study and hard work. We felt "ready" to walk across the stage, receive our diplomas, and celebrate our achievements. But there was also a little fear and trembling as we thought about our upcoming ventures into the unknown—new schools, college courses, dormitory life, unfamiliar faces, and adjusting to new schedules and routines.

As that summer drew to a close, my boyfriend and I prepared to go off to different schools. We realized that the separation would be difficult, but we were determined to carry on our relationship through letters, phone calls, and greatly anticipated reunions during holidays and semester breaks.

Once the fall semester got underway, however, each of us became involved in studying, writing term papers, and participating in extracurricular activities. The days became busier and more scheduled. Free time became almost non-existent. Gradually our letters and phone calls drifted off into oblivion. We had very little contact with each other for several months.

Before long, the Christmas season was upon us. After a rigorous week of meeting deadlines for assignments and taking final exams, I headed home for the holidays. My thoughts focused on my family, decorating our house, baking cookies, buying gifts, and carrying out the traditions which had meant so much to me through the years.

A few nights after arriving home, my boyfriend and I met for dinner. We were excited to see each other again, but after only a few minutes, our conversation became awkward and uncomfortable, with longer and longer periods of silence. Our laughter seemed forced and insincere. It soon became obvious to both of us that we had drifted apart. Our once close relationship had suffered from lack of attention and communication. After four months of living in separate worlds, it was impossible to simply pick up where we had left off.

This painful experience taught me a memorable lesson about personal relationships, not only with regard to friends, but also, and more importantly, with respect to God. Frequent communication is crucial in developing and maintaining quality relationships.

In this lesson, Daniel is described as a faithful servant who constantly followed the law of his God (cf. 6:4,5). He maintained his daily prayer and devotional routine in spite of the life-threatening ordinance which King Darius had signed (6:10). His personal relationship with God had earned him the reputation of being a man with the spirit of the holy gods, a man of light, understanding, knowledge, and great wisdom (5:11,12).

May Daniel's faithfulness and perseverance inspire us all to commit a portion of each day to prayer and loving service to God.

LESSON 7
Daniel 7–9

A Review of History—
Daniel's First Three Visions

God, Help me to have a clear vision of who You are; of who I am in You; of the good works You have for me to do. AMEN.

In our studies so far of the Book of Daniel we have looked closely at several short stories featuring Daniel (Belteshazzar), Hananiah (Shadrach), Misha-el (Meshach), and Azariah (Abednego), the four young Jewish refugee captives who achieved recognition and prominence in the court of Nebuchadnezzar of Babylon. In these stories we rediscovered God's central message for His people—faithfulness and obedience will be rewarded even though for a time events may seem to offer no hope. Here was a message for the pious Jews—the Hasidim—who were the Daniel writer's first readers, that they must be faithful to the Law at all costs. They saw in this message that they would be delivered and that God's rule and kingdom would last but the earthly kingdoms ruled by treacherous tyrants would perish and pass off the scene.

Earlier we saw those earthly kingdoms symbolized in Nebuchadnezzar's dream by the huge statue with the head of gold, chest and arms of silver, an abdomen of brass, legs of iron, and feet of iron mixed with clay. We understand that the proper interpretation of the symbolism identifies the head of gold with Babylon, the chest and arms of silver with Media, the abdomen of brass with Persia, the legs of iron with Greece, and the feet of iron mixed with clay with the Hellenistic kingdoms of Syria and Egypt.

Now as we move into the second half of the Book of Daniel we sense a distinct change of pace and perspective. Here the writing moves from third person to first. And here we have the account of Daniel's four visions or dreams that trace the overthrow of nations that have dominated world history and ruled with brutal and oppressive practices. These visions or dreams can be very confusing to those of us who live in the closing years of the twentieth century and are accustomed to reading an entirely different kind of literature. So at this point you may find it helpful to reread those paragraphs in the Preface to these lessons under the subheads entitled "A Special Type of Literature: Apocalyptic" and "Prophecy in a New Idiom."

Daniel's Vision of Four Empires (7:1–28)

In the world and experience of the Old Testament, visions and dreams were considered vehicles of divine revelation. And this first vision of Daniel's seems to have a definite relationship to Nebuchadnezzar's dream in which he saw the huge image described in Daniel 2 and the ultimate establishment of the rule of God on earth.

The Four Symbolic Animals (Beasts)

As we've already mentioned, apocalyptic literature is rich in symbolism. And as we move into our discussion of this first vision of Daniel, we are immediately introduced to the four symbolic animals that Daniel saw. First, the Daniel writer tells us that these four beasts emerged from the deep sea. In ancient thought the turbulent waters of the sea—the hostile watery chaos—was the place of evil. The sea was the home of all sorts of dreadful and fearsome monsters. And apparently, as it is used here in Daniel's vision, the sea symbolizes the agitated and frenzied world of the human race that is hostile to God and His chosen people.

It was out of this chaos, this place of evil, that "four great beasts came up . . . diverse [each one

157

different] one from another" (7:3). First, there was a lion with eagle's wings (7:4). The second beast is described "like to a bear . . . and it had three ribs in the mouth [also might be translated "fangs"]" (7:5). The third animal was "like a leopard, which had upon the back of it four wings . . . also four heads" (7:6). And the fourth animal is described as the most terrible of all with "great iron teeth" and ten horns. And to complete the description, the Daniel writer speaks of a small horn which appeared and uprooted three of the original ten, "in this horn were eyes like the eyes of man, and a mouth speaking great things" (7:8b).

It is generally accepted that these four animals were symbolic of four great empires—Babylon, the lion with eagle's wings; Media, the bear; Persia, the leopard with four wings and four heads; and the fourth beast with the ten horns, symbolized the Greek (Hellenistic) or Seleucid empires. Finally, the little horn quite likely symbolizes Antiochus IV.

While the imagery here seems weird to us, we are familiar with animal or bird symbolism representing nations even today. For example, the eagle is a symbol associated with the United States of America. And the bear is a symbol associated with Russia. But at this point it is important that we not get so bogged down by the imagery that we lose sight of the truly great message—the kingdoms and nations of this world may rise and seem invincible, but God's kingdom will prevail in the long run; God is in charge of our universe—from the beginning of time to the end, whenever that will be. Other of the Old Testament prophets had glimpses of this future, but it was Daniel who had a sustained vision of the future and of God's kingdom.

It is truly sad that this magnificent Book of Daniel has been trivialized in two different ways. First, there are those who consider it so ridiculous, too fantastic to be taken seriously—merely a work of science fiction. And, second, there are those who use it as a vehicle for all sorts of speculation when it comes to describing and dating the time of the end. However, the primary intent of this wonderful and imaginative piece of writing is to present God's revelation in symbolic form.

As we move now through the rest of the Daniel story we will be greatly encouraged to persevere and hope. The message of the Book of Daniel was not exhausted in the second century B.C., or at the destruction of Jerusalem in A.D. 70, or under the persecution launched by the Roman emperor Domitian in A.D. 95. And it will not be outdated in A.D. 1995 or even in A.D. 2095. It looks ultimately ahead to the End Time, and is a constant and ongoing source of hope for the people of God in all time.

There has been a persistent march of tyrants in most every century who have attempted to subject people to their insanities. Our twentieth century has been ravaged by two world wars plus a seemingly never-ending series of regional "police actions" and conflicts, instigated by power-hungry despots. Russia and eastern Europe and Asia felt the madness of Stalin. And both the eastern and western world felt the insanity of Adolph Hitler.

In every instance Christians have been called upon to resist these power hungry tyrants. Albert Einstein, speaking of Hitler's rise to power, said that when persecution and evil began to spread across Germany, he looked first to the great universities for opposition, but they were soon neutralized. Then he looked hopefully to the press, but they were soon suppressed. It was only in the Christian churches that men like the Bonhoeffer brothers and Helmut Thielicke dared to stand up for the rights of truth and freedom. Our century has seen a time of mad dictators, and in every instance Christians have been looked to for leadership in opposing them in the name of our God.

The great lesson we learn as people of faith is that our God is ultimately in charge. Power hungry men with the capability of persuading the masses may seem to prevail for a time. Benito Mussolini ruled as the Fascist dictator of Italy from 1922 until 1943. It appeared as if nothing could stop him, and yet he died an ignominious death in utter defeat. Adolph

A Ring of Hope

Hitler, Chancellor and dictator of Germany from 1933 to 1945, threatened the entire world and launched the Holocaust that cost the lives of six million Jews gave every indication of being unstoppable. Yet his seemingly invincible armies were defeated by the Allied forces and he died in an underground bunker.

Joseph Stalin, Secretary General of the Communist party in Russia from 1922 to 1953, ruthlessly murdered millions of his countrymen in his struggle for total power, and the threat of communism moved out across the world inflicting outrageously cruel suppression on millions. And in China there was Mao Tse-tung who ruled China with an iron hand from 1943 until his death.

To many people it could have seemed as if the forces of evil and the disciples of atheistic ideologies had finally won out. But the 1980s have witnessed a staggering breakdown of Communism in Russia, Poland, and the rest of Europe. To Germans, east and west, the Berlin wall, that ugly symbol of suppression, has been peacefully breached and rendered useless. And we've seen stirrings of things to come in China. In the sixth and second centuries B.C., despots threatened the world, even as they have in the twentieth century A.D., but in every era the people of God have been firm in their stand against evil. God is in charge!

The Divine Judge: The Ancient of Days

After that remarkable vision of history had passed before Daniel's eyes, the scene suddenly shifts and he saw a vision of God (7:9–12). In the vision Daniel saw that seats for a judgment court were in place, and an aged judge, "the Ancient of days," with a white robe and white hair took his place, "his throne was like the fiery flame, and his wheels as burning fire" (7:9b). The symbolism of fire and judgment is familiar throughout our Old Testament.

Pictured in this vision with the heavenly court was God Almighty as Judge, and it is one of the most splendid pictures of God in all the Old Testament. God was indeed a majestic and venerable figure. His white clothes symbolized His purity. His white hair spoke of His eternal being, and His fiery throne (see

Ezek. 1 & 10) symbolized His right to judge and His power to purify (see Rev. 1).

As the crowd viewed the court scene, the books of records were open—apparently in them was recorded the evil deeds of the four animal kingdoms. Here we see the "Ancient of days," presiding over the heavenly council at the Last Judgment, sentencing the fourth kingdom to destruction. The lesson for the first readers of Daniel, and for us, is that a persecuting tyrant is under condemnation of God. Daniel's first readers saw this as the inevitable end of Antiochus IV and the destruction of the Seleucid dynasty. The other three animal kingdoms also fell under God's judgment even though they were spared the fate of the fourth kingdom.

One Like the Son of Man

Once again, the scene shifts. The beasts have been judged and the fourth beast destroyed. Now in his vision Daniel sees "one like the Son of man" appear on the heavenly stage, a human being in contrast to the beasts (7:13–14). Power and authority were given to him, along with the assurance that his kingdom would endure.

Jesus often referred to Himself as "the Son of Man" and was undoubtedly deeply influenced by the imagery and message of Daniel 7. He saw Himself as embodying in His work, life, death, and resurrection the coming kingdom of Daniel's prophecy. In the Old Testament there are three distinct savior figures—the Messiah, the Suffering Servant, and the Son of Man. In the religion of Judaism these three figures were kept distinct, but Jesus blended them into one to explain His own uniqueness. As the Suffering Servant, Jesus was exalted to the glorious Son of Man position where He was given the eternal kingdom of God.

The Interpretation

Next we hear Daniel saying, "I Daniel was grieved in my spirit in the midst of my body, and the visions of my head troubled me." It is little wonder that Daniel was puzzled and alarmed by what he had seen and heard. So he asked one of the angelic attendants to the Ancient of days what all of this meant (7:15–16). In response, the angel explained that the four animals represented the four kings who were the heads of four kingdoms. These would pass off the scene, but only "the saints of the most High" would prevail.

But apparently Daniel wasn't satisfied, for he now asks for more information, especially about the fourth beast or kingdom (7:19–22). Again the angel messenger responds with the description of that fourth kingdom, the most terrible of all, who would "devour the whole earth, and . . . tread it down, and break it in pieces" (7:23).

As we've indicated already, there is a general consensus that this fourth kingdom is the one founded by Alexander the Great. Then upon Alexander's death (327 B.C.) the empire was divided and followed by a succession of kings (the ten horns). The focus of the vision was on the boastful "little horn" (7:20) who is generally identified as Antiochus IV who made his way to the throne at the expense of three others. It was Antiochus who became the arch-enemy of God and of the Jews, and who was guilty of slaughtering all the Jews who refused to go along with his repressive and sinful measures. But then comes the promise that even though Antiochus would seem to succeed for a time, his arrogant and devastating rule would indeed come to an end and the people of God would prevail (7:23–28).

Daniel's Vision of the End Time (8:1–27)

As we move into this next part of our lesson, we once again are confronted with a vision that features animal figures. And as we look more closely upon this scene, we realize the theme is a continuation of what we saw in Chapter 7. There has been a lapse of time between the visions, but the message of hope and deliverance for God's people is central.

Daniel's Vision of the Ram and the He-goat

First we're told that two years has elapsed between Daniel's first vision as seen in Chapter 7 and the vision that occurs at this point. Next, we're told that Daniel either saw himself or was at Shushan (Susa), the capital of Elam (southwestern Iran). Shushan would become the winter residence of the future Persian kings (8:1–2).

The vision opens with Daniel seeing a ram, the

symbol of Medo-Persian power, standing by the river. Next we're told that the ram "had two horns: and the two horns were high; but one was higher than the other, and the higher came up last" (8:3). The short horn represented the Median kingdom and the longer horn symbolized the Persian empire. In the vision the ram was mighty and fierce and is described as moving rapidly "westward, and northward, and southward," descriptive of the Persian military campaigns (8:4).

While the ram was at the height of its conquest, the scene shifts and Daniel comments, "And as I was considering, behold, an he-goat came from the west on the face of the whole earth, and touched not the ground: and the goat had a notable horn between his eyes" (8:5). In colorful picture language we're being told that the goat came rampaging out of the west—Europe—and was traveling so fast that its feet hardly touched the ground.

Now follows the picture of the fast moving and powerful goat attacking the ram with fury and completely defeating it (8:6–7). In the scene we have a picture of Alexander the Great's rapid and victorious career as he crushed Darius III, the last Persian king, and conquered the Persian empire (334–323 B.C.). Alexander's march across the ancient Middle East had by the time of his early death subdued all of that part of the world.

But history reveals that Alexander's pride and arrogance led to his downfall. Having conquered the world of his day, he died while still a young man, sighing for more worlds to conquer. Since Alexander had no son to succeed him, his empire went to four of his generals—Cassander (Greece), Lysimachus (Anatolia), Seleucus (Syria and Mesopotamia), and Ptolemy (Egypt). Note the wording of verse 8.

The Little Horn

The author of the Book of Daniel quickly moved the drama of history to the urgent present in which we believe he was living and the campaign of Antiochus IV against Palestine (8:9–12). Antiochus IV (175–164 B.C.) was the eighth of the Syrian line, and his ambition was to conquer Egypt and make all of his subjects submit to the pagan Greek religion.

Antiochus occupies center stage in the vision now as we are given a picture of his repressive measures at the height of the Maccabean revolt (168–165 B.C.).

The reference to the "little horn" casting down some of the "stars" (8:10) probably has to do with the attack that Antiochus made against the heathen religions in his empire in his effort to force everyone to worship the Greek gods and goddesses. Then we learn that Antiochus launched his attack on the stronghold of God—"the prince of the host"—by ravaging the Jerusalem Temple and suspending the regular morning and evening sacrifices (Exod. 29:39ff.). Next, he removed the sacred altar from the Temple and erected an altar to the Greek god Zeus. Finally, we're told that he "cast down the truth to the ground" (8:12). He wiped out the Jewish Law, forced the Jews to give up the rite of circumcision, stop reading their Scriptures, and discontinue all sacrifices and holy days. And, finally, we're told that he compounded the humiliation of the Jews by forcing them to eat pork and sacrifice ritually unclean animals. History tells us that the Jews resisted and were slaughtered by the thousands. It looked at that point as if nothing could stop the ruthless Antiochus and that true religion had failed.

But then we see that God had set a limit to the blasphemous arrogance of Antiochus (8:13–14). In the vision Daniel now hears two angels talking about how long the "transgression of desolation" would last—how long would it be before relief would come? And in response the answer comes—after two thousand three hundred morning and evening sacrifices, or 1,150 days. In other words, it would not be long before this time of madness would end.

The Interpretation of the Second Vision

While we have the benefit of centuries of interpretation, Daniel did not have this luxury. So it is not surprising that as Daniel reflected over what he had seen, he was puzzled. What did it all mean (8:15)? In response to his quandary we're told that an angel figure appeared before him and was instructed to give Daniel the interpretation. We're told the angel's name was Gabriel, and this identifies him as one of the seven archangels—the other six being Uriel, Michael, Remiel, Raphael, Saraquel, and Raguel.

This is the first mention of Gabriel in the Old Testament Scriptures. He is mentioned one more time in the Book of Daniel, and was, of course, the Lord's messenger to Zacharias and to Mary (Luke 1:19, 26). And his name appears quite often in other Jewish writings in the intertestament period. In fact, it was during this Greek period that a prolific angelic tradition emerged among the Jews. The angels were known to be God's representatives to guard His heavenly throne, act as His messengers, serve as guides for people, and reveal God's secret intentions.

The Daniel writer next tells us that when the angel figure appeared, Daniel was awestruck—so paralyzed with fright that he fell into a trancelike sleep (8:17–25). It was then Daniel was told that his vision had to do with a future "End Time"—the time when the persecutions instigated by Antiochus IV would end and the Jews would triumph. The "time of the end" in apocalyptic literature referred to that future golden age of peace and prosperity under God's rule.

Then follows the explanation of the various features of the vision. The language is so explicit that the meaning couldn't be missed. Media, Persia, and Greece are referred to briefly (8:20–21). Then comes Antiochus in whom evil and wickedness reached its peak. He is described as defiant, designing, crafty, destructive, boastful, and prosperous—constantly fighting against God and His people.

Antiochus is described in our Scripture lesson as having a "fierce countenance," indicating his insolence and harshness toward the Jews and their God (8:23b). And the phrase "understanding dark sentences" (8:23c) points to his skill in political intrigue, his basic duplicity in language, and his ability to trick his way to the fulfillment of his goals. History tells us that Antiochus liquidated his opponents with cunning and deceit.

For example, in 168 B.C. Antiochus sent his general Appolonius to Jerusalem on a pretended mission of peace. But once the city had been lulled to quiet with peace talk Appolonius turned his Greek army loose

A view of a wall in Babylon containing the symbol of Marduk, the chief god in Babylon. Marduk's accession to the position of chief god is described in the Enuma elish, *the Babylonian creation story.*

on the Jews and killed hundreds of them. It was then the Temple was sacked and desecrated by Zeus worship in the Holy of Holies. This desecration was branded into the memory of Jews forever.

Then comes the grand promise; Antiochus "shall be broken without hand" (8:25c). In other words, Antiochus will be destroyed, but not by human hands. God would deal with him as he deserved. And just a year later, in 164 B.C., Antiochus died a madman on an expedition to Persia. Here was a man whose genius was mixed with insanity. John Milton, the English poet, said, "The mind is its own place, and in itself can make a Heaven of Hell, a Hell of Heaven." In truth, Antiochus was a man whose mind was in ruins. His evil genius was finally brought in check by God.

The message of hope was clear. Even as the supernatural mountain shattered the metal image in Chapter 2, and as the Ancient of days stopped the ravaging beast in Chapter 7, so God would indeed rescue His people from Antiochus. And it is Antiochus who became the model for the Antichrist—the belief that arose in later Christian times that an evil figure would arise at the End Time to do battle with God Himself. Antiochus, then, is the figure behind every Antichrist of any century who plays the role of oppressor—the personification of wickedness and evil who will ultimately be overcome by God.

Enormous energy has been wasted over the years in an effort to identify the Antichrist. But perceptive Christians have recognized in tyrants from Nero to Hitler the long shadow of Antiochus. Late-twentieth-century and twenty-first century Christians have every right to be alert to the insidious forces of evil in people and in institutions that try to play God. But our living hope comes in the assurance that a time is coming that will signal the end of evil and that God will establish His rule on earth through Jesus Christ.

Finally, Daniel was assured by Gabriel (8:26–27) that the vision of the End Time was true, and this is what the author wanted his readers in 165 B.C. to rely on. It was then the vision would be disclosed. This was a favorite literary device of apocalyptic writers—to address a predictive message from a past age that was to be kept hidden until it was needed. So, the original readers of the Book of Daniel knew they were not being deceived, but instead they were being led to see that the God who controlled past history also controlled history in their own time. Instead of being "fooled," the original readers of Daniel would have felt encouraged. They knew that the past could give a perspective on their present crisis, so they welcomed the message of Daniel. And the message belongs to the people of God in every century—while there are those who would thwart the plans of God, His rule is eternal; He is the God of history.

Those who suffer understand what hope is. Daniel knew that God could transform the worst of troubles into triumph. Even as nature can take the unattractive and convert it into a thing of beauty. We can take black coal and produce beautiful synthetics from it. In the far north, trees must endure high winds and ice storms, but they grow into strong, hard wood. Faith in God gives life a similar transforming power—the power to turn the ugly into something inspiring.

Simon Kenton (1755–1836), famous frontier scout, friend of Daniel Boone, and implacable foe of the Indians in the dark and bloody ground of the Ohio River Valley, had no faith in God. But on Wednesday, October 26, 1808, at a camp meeting led by a Methodist minister named Bennett Maxey, he confessed his sins and his ruthless killing and became a Christian. The first thing that Kenton did was to lay down his rifle. Carrying the six foot long flintlock gun cradled in his arm had been a habit since he was a boy, and he was now fifty-five years old. To give up the death-dealing weapon was not an easy change to make. As a kind of compromise, he fashioned a fine staff over five feet in length and he carried this with him wherever he went, grasping it about a foot from its upper end. From then on everyone knew that Simon Kenton was a transformed man of faith. If anyone abused his friendship, he might crack them over the head with his stick, but he would not kill them as he had killed so many in the past.

Daniel's Vision of the Seventy Weeks (9:1–27)

As we have seen in our studies so far, it is difficult for our modern minds to grasp the meaning of apocalyptic writing. Our western pragmatic minds run along quite different tracks from our spiritual ancestors between the sixth and the first centuries B.C. Also we have acknowledged that there are different viewpoints among responsible interpreters of the Book of Daniel. We respect these differences; however, for the purpose of our study here, we have pursued the interpretive direction widely held by the majority of present-day scholars.

Daniel's Study of Jeremiah's Prophecy

This part of our Scripture lesson opens with the Daniel author taking us back to the time of Darius—a time when the Jews had high hopes of complete deliverance from their exile and foreign oppression. And in this opening scene we find Daniel puzzling over Jeremiah's prophecy that restoration would be completed after a period of seventy years (Jer. 25:11–12; 29:10). You will remember that Jeremiah preached as a prophet between approximately 625 to 575 B.C. But from the standpoint of the author of the Book of Daniel, who we presume to be writing in the second century B.C., the "exile" was not complete, for the Jews were still an oppressed people. Jeremiah's seventy years had stretched into centuries. But as we will see further on in this lesson, a new understanding of Jeremiah's seventy years was needed. A little later we will discover that what is meant was that the seventy years represented seventy weeks of years ($70 \times 7 = 490$ years).

Daniel's Prayer for His People

At this point, though, the Daniel writer interrupts the narrative with a beautiful prayer by Daniel (9:3–19). First, we see Daniel preparing himself for prayer "with fasting, and sackcloth, and ashes" (9:3). In his preparation to meet God he got ready physically, mentally, and spiritually. Then when he was prepared, he probably used a liturgical prayer that has been long used in the Temple or synagogue. When he prayed "O Lord, the great and dreadful God, keeping the covenant and mercy to them that love him, and to them that keep his commandments," he focused on the very heart of the Jewish faith (9:4). God graciously and lovingly chose Israel to be His special people, and they were to display loyal love for Him by keeping His commandments.

But then Daniel confessed Israel's persistent covenant disloyalty (9:5), and in particular their unwillingness to listen to God's messengers, the prophets (9:6). Because of their disobedience and sinfulness, they had been subdued and driven into exile—Israel in the north in 922 B.C., and Judah in the south in 587 B.C. And because of their treachery, all of God's people were oppressed and captive (9:7). In short, the people of Israel had brought about their own destruction, and because of their lack of repentance their calamities continued (9:8–14).

Then, having confessed the sins of the Jewish people, Daniel began to plead with God to give His people speedy relief based on His steadfast and gracious goodness. The Daniel author directs this petition to God both for the exiles in Babylon (538 B.C.), and his compatriots who were suffering under Antiochus IV (165 B.C.). Daniel remembers how God had graciously saved his ancestors at the time of the Exodus from Egypt (9:15). Now he prays that God will deliver the city of Jerusalem (9:16–18). Nebuchadnezzar had destroyed the city in 587 B.C., and now centuries later Antiochus IV continued to desecrate it. It was clear that the sinful people of Israel had no personal grounds for relief, "but for thy great mercies," Daniel called on God for help. After all, it is by God's mercy that we are delivered from whatever kind of slavery entraps us, not by any particular merit of ours. Finally, the prayer is concluded by reminding God that the Jews were His chosen people and Jerusalem was His city and that He had much invested in them, including His honor (9:18–19).

The Interpretation

Even before he had concluded his prayer, God had already set in motion the means whereby Daniel would learn the hidden meaning of Jeremiah's prophecy. God dispatched Gabriel, the archangel, to explain what it all meant. The explanation begins with a great affirmation of Daniel, "thou art great beloved" (9:23a). Then Gabriel goes on to explain that Jeremiah's seventy weeks were seventy weeks of seven years each, or 490 years, and at the end of that time God would usher in a new day. That would be a day of righteousness and peace when the altar Antiochus had desecrated would be restored and reconsecrated (9:24).

Gabriel next (9:25–27) lays out before Daniel an explanation of the divisions of time within the seventy week-years and winds up with what we believe to be the last week of seven years covered by the reign of Antiochus IV.

The use of the term *Messiah* in our King James text (verses 25 and 26) is generally believed to be a mistranslation. A better translation would be "the anointed one" or "prince"—terms used for the High Priest after the exile. In the New Testament the term *Messiah* has Christological meaning and is a technical term for the future ideal King. However, the term is not used in that sense in the Book of Daniel.

During the first half of this "last week" (171–168 B.C.), Antiochus showed some lenience toward the Jews who were sympathetic to Greek ideas. But during the last half of the week (168–164 B.C.), the time in which we believe the author of the Book of Daniel was living and writing, he unleashed general Apollonius on Jerusalem. It was then Jews were slaughtered and the Temple was violated by the altar to Zeus. The "abomination" in verse 27 probably refers to Zeus—the same as the Baal Shamayim or "Lord of Heaven" worshiped by the pagans. The pious Jews structured a religious pun by changing the name Baal to "abomination" *(Shiqquts)* and Shamayim *(shomen),* creating the contemptuous title, "abomination of desolation" (Matt. 24:15).

Apparently the author of the Book of Daniel finished writing his book some months before the Temple was finally cleansed and restored and before Antiochus died. But he lived and wrote with the firm conviction that God would soon be victorious. According to his view, history followed a prearranged timetable in which the length of each period was set by God. At first this might strike us as too predetermined, but it is important we understand that the author had the deep conviction that God was in control of events.

As we view this, the Daniel writer believed he was living in the second half of that last week of years. From his perspective the clock was about to strike midnight, time was running out, and God was about to depose Antiochus IV. The countdown on God's clock and calendar was almost over, and the End Time was near. This was no mechanical theory of predestination but a lively faith that God was in control of history. Indeed, we live in "His-story."

Daniel for Me

At the time the Daniel author was writing he didn't have the faintest idea that he was producing Scripture or that by God's providence he would become an inspiring model for millions in later centuries. As I have reflected on this, I have been reminded of my great-great Uncle Thomas who died in 1844 at the age of thirty-eight.

My first bit of information about Uncle Thomas was that he had been bitten by a rabid dog and had died an excruciating and painful death a month later. Some years ago, it fell my lot as the family archivist and genealogist to study Uncle Thomas' papers to learn more about him and his seemingly strange behavior during his final days.

Slowly I began to put the pieces together and the picture began to make sense. Apparently after Thomas was bitten by the mad dog he realized he was doomed, so he sprang into action with grim resolution and careful planning. He was determined to provide for his pregnant wife Narcissa and their six other children, all under thirteen years of age.

Thomas's final act of preparation was to hurry to Charleston, South Carolina, over two hundred miles away, to buy a wagon load of supplies for his family. He probably galloped his horse almost to death during that desperate ride. Upon arrival in Charleston, he quickly bought his supplies, a wagon, and a fresh team of horses and headed home as fast as possible. His was a test of sheer will power, and before he got close to home hemorrhaging had already begun in his brain. And when he finally crossed the bridge leading to his property he was hallucinating so badly that he could hardly see his house.

Not long after arriving home he died in madness and pain, tied down to his own bed with ropes. However, a few days before his sanity left him completely he had called in a lawyer to make out his final will. And in that will he confessed his faith in God and made meticulous plans for the care of his family. I could find no indication that he ever complained or showed the least sign of self-pity. Rather he spent his last days thinking of others.

Uncle Thomas's implacable resolution, his strong sense of duty, his faith in God, his love for Narcissa and their little children, his iron determination to make every minute count has been an inspiration to me ever since I was able to piece together his story. He never knew what a legacy he was leaving to me over a century later.

Narcissa buried Uncle Thomas on a little hill in a cluster of oak trees that looked down a beautiful sloping valley toward their home. I have sat by that grave, patted the tombstone, and said silently, "Thank you, Uncle, for all you tried to do. You have left me a good model." In a similar manner, I, along with untold multitudes of believers who have read the Book of Daniel, have said, "Thank you, Daniel, for giving me courage and hope in times of trouble. You have left me a good model of faith in God when my own courage has been weak."

Father, How is my life a model for others? What do I, by my actions and attitudes, encourage others to do—or avoid? Help me to be like Daniel, who is still an example today to be followed. AMEN.

WHAT THIS SCRIPTURE MEANS TO ME
Daniel 7—9

The neighborhood in Detroit, Michigan, where I grew up was a wonderful place. I can't remember a time when I didn't have something to do or somewhere to go with a neighborhood friend. And in spite of the wide spectrum of ages represented by the many children on our city block, we managed to get along fairly well . . . until Mark's family moved into the house down the street.

It was absolutely amazing to witness the drastic change in group dynamics which resulted from one boy's entrance into our neighborhood. From "day one," Mark's presence in any activity—regardless of the size of the group—spelled Trouble with a capital T. He pestered young children unmercifully by pulling their hair, making faces, or jabbing and poking at them. With his peers, he invariably started fist fights and wrestling matches, often resulting in bloody noses or scraped arms and legs. Mark was a bully in every sense of the word.

And then, quite unexpectedly, Linda drastically altered the situation. No one *ever* expected quiet, reserved Linda to have the impact she did.

One damp and frigid winter morning, several of us spontaneously gathered in front of my house. There had been a snowstorm the previous day, followed by rain and sleet which had frozen during the night. The snowy lawns were thus covered by a quarter-inch layer of ice. We discovered that by carefully wedging our mittened hands between the ice and snow, we could lift up large sections of ice. We then held these way over our heads and watched them smash into hundreds of pieces when we dropped them onto the sidewalk.

Before long, Mark's familiar frame could be seen walking toward us. Our laughter and excitement immediately disappeared. We all stood in motionless silence as this troublemaker approached, waiting uncomfortably to see who would be "attacked" first. Mark had been watching us lifting up the sheets of ice, and he quickly challenged us to a contest. Not wanting to aggravate him, we slowly and quietly walked to untrodden sections of the yard and stooped down to scrape up our individual "entries." Then, just as slowly and quietly, we returned to the sidewalk, awaiting "judgment." Then, lo and behold, Linda's hands gripped an enormous slab of ice, obviously larger than Mark's. Someone gasped. Others held their breath, waiting to see the "loser's" reaction.

We watched in horror as Mark threw down his piece and stomped over to where Linda stood with both hands still supporting her prize-winning ice like a tray of fine crystal. She didn't budge an inch. She just stared at his red, angry face. Suddenly Mark lunged forward, his chest pushing the icy platform into Linda's chin and neck.

Without a word or sideways glance, Linda grasped the ice firmly, and shoved it right back at Mark, hitting him squarely on the mouth. The force of it made him lose his balance. He plunged awkwardly into the crunchy snow, tears in his eyes, blood on his lips, and a dazed and disbelieving expression on his face. Finally, finally, justice had prevailed.

These chapters in Daniel contain several vivid images of power and strength. But for me, the underlying theme is one of hope and encouragement. For in God's time, the humble and seemingly weak "saints of the Most High" (7:18, 7:27) *will* prevail against those who magnify and exalt themselves (8:1–4, 8:8, 8:11, 8:25). In spite of suffering and temporary setbacks, God's people must remain faithful. We must, to quote a recent presidential hopeful, "never surrender, and never give up. We must keep hope alive, keep hope alive, keep hope alive."

LESSON 8
Daniel 10–12

A Vision of the End Time: A Portrait of the Last Days

Father, It's comforting to know that You are the God who sees me: I'm never out of Your view. You provide for my needs and rescue me fully. AMEN.

What We Have Seen

So far we have seen how the author of the Book of Daniel used the wide sweep of history from the exile in Babylon to the time of Antiochus IV in the second century B.C. to get at the relationship between God and events. In the seventh chapter of Daniel the author portrayed history as a concentration of disorder with the images of four strange and fearsome animals emerging onto the seashore. This suggested to us that while God is in charge of history, the process may at times be unsavory, dark, disturbing, and with no apparent meaning.

In the eighth chapter of Daniel we saw history after the Hebrew exile described as an experience of God's wrath in which aggressive kings (or national powers) fought each other like wild animals. Each arrogant empire aroused the envy of another which challenged and defeated it. It wasn't that God imposed this pattern, but that each nation determined its own destiny. Israel was caught in this harsh pattern of affliction and experienced, not God's comfort, but God's absence.

In the ninth chapter of Daniel we saw Israel's exile and desolation continuing over centuries, way beyond Jeremiah's understanding of the seventy years. We also saw how the Archangel Gabriel interpreted the seventy-year period as a symbolic time that was under God's control. According to our understanding of the Book of Daniel, this End Time of Israel's period of severe suffering would soon be over.

What We Will See

Now, in Chapters 10, 11, and 12 of Daniel we see the fourth and last vision of the book. Like the previous three it concerns the Last Days and the events leading up to them. It is one vision and is given special emphasis by its length and its location at the end of the book. This fourth vision covers the same

A Bedouin family among the ruins of ancient Babylon. While modern day Iraq is permitting a certain amount of restoration work, today's Babylon is bleak and bears little resemblance to the splendor of the ancient city.

ground as the other three but with more historical details—more about the suffering of the Jews in the second century B.C., and more about their vindication at the End Time.

In Chapter 10, we have the Prologue introducing the vision. The vision proper and its interpretation follows in Chapter 11. Here we are given the events of secular history in great detail only to show us how events are essentially meaningless and insignificant in themselves. The history of the Jews after their return from exile only had meaning in the light of revelation, since God's purposes cannot be determined from history itself. In Chapter 12 we have the Epilogue—a portrait of the End Time in which we have a message of hope about those whom death had seemed to rob of a chance to share in God's kingdom. The vision as a whole links Israel's leaders with the same trials described in Chapters 1–6 of the Book of Daniel and challenges them to be as steadfast as the heroes in those wisdom stories. Daniel-like leadership and courage is held up as a model of steadfastness and faithfulness.

Prologue: Daniel is Told of the Future of Persia and Greece (10:1–21)

The scene opens with the Daniel writer setting the stage, "In the third year of Cyrus King of Persia [535 B.C.] a thing was revealed unto Daniel, whose name was called Belteshazzar; and the thing was true, but the time appointed was long: and he understood the thing, and had understanding of the vision" (10:1). It is apparent that Daniel here received a divine revelation that laid out before him all of history from the time of Cyrus to the second century B.C. and beyond. It was made clear that this would be a time of desperate conflict and struggle.

The Heavenly Messenger

We next learn that in preparing for the promised vision Daniel went into a three-week period of mourning and fasting, during which he focused his mind on the message that was to come (10:2–3). Immediately after this time of preparation we're told that on the twenty-fourth day of Passover he was standing on the bank of the Tigris River when he was suddenly confronted by a dazzling supernatural figure—quite likely the angel Gabriel in human form

(10:4–9). This part of the vision was like Ezekiel's (Ezek. 1) or Saul's (Acts 9). Daniel was paralyzed with fear and his companions, keenly aware that something special was happening, ran and hid themselves (10:7). Only Daniel saw the ecstatic vision, and he was completely immobilized by it (10:8). We're further told that while he heard the angel's words, he couldn't distinguish what was being said while he lay in the dust (10:9).

The Heavenly Conflict

While Daniel was lying there on the ground, he felt the touch of a friendly hand—probably Gabriel's—that helped him up to his knees, and heard two statements that must have electrified him. First, Gabriel said Daniel was "a man greatly beloved." Then came the reassuring words, "Fear not" (10:11–12). This scene reminds us of Jesus, who so frequently in His ministry touched people—and they were healed; who again and again said, "Fear not" to troubled people. There is something therapeutic about a tender and loving touch accompanied by quiet words that calm our fears. What a marvelous ministry we can all have through a touch and words of love.

Following this reassuring scene, we read that the angel visitor assured Daniel that the future would be explained. Gabriel went on to explain to Daniel that "the prince [the angel] of the kingdom of Persia withstood me one and twenty days: but, lo, Michael, one of the chief princes [angels], came to help me; and I remained there with the kings of Persia" (10:13). From these words we gather that the guardian angel of Persia had attempted to stop Gabriel from getting to Daniel, but Michael, the patron angel of the Jews, had appeared on the scene to help Gabriel.

While this may seem strange to us, it would have been quite familiar to the first readers of Daniel. They believed that patron angels determined the destinies of individual nations. As a matter of fact, it was during this period that the whole idea of angelic presences became so much a part of the Jewish religion. By the time of the Maccabees in the second and first century B.C. the doctrine had become developed to where it was believed that whatever happened on earth had a counterpart in heaven. Wars fought on earth were reflected by the wars fought among the guardian angels in heaven, and one nation defeated another because one army of angels defeated the other in heaven. The implication of this belief was that both human decisions and heavenly powers share in shaping the events of earthly history.

But while Gabriel had been delayed three weeks, he now makes it clear that he had come to enlighten Daniel about the distant future—that time of the End when Antiochus IV would move off the scene and the historic process would reach its climax (10:14). In response Daniel, like Ezekiel, was so overcome with wonder and amazement that he lost his faculties a second time and was unable to speak. Once again, though, the angel revived him and he was able to respond to God (10:15–17).

The Nature of God's Revelation

Chapter 10 consistently affirms that the message to Daniel was a revelation from God brought by heavenly beings (angels). This implies several things. First, there is a real contact between heaven and earth, and God reveals Himself when we earnestly seek Him. Second, a claim to have a revelation from God doesn't make it so just because we or someone else claims it is so. God gives His revelation to people of proven discernment and faithfulness such as Daniel.

Third, our personal insight alone is not enough to make our message a divine revelation, simply because revelation must be in large part a piece of Scriptural exposition. We can't be out of line with what is already given in the Bible and have a true message from God. Fourth, in the spirit of the Bible we can reapply the Scriptures to our own current situation as the author of Daniel reapplied Scripture to Antiochus and the promised destiny of conservative Jews. Fifth, we can be certain that if our revelation is from God it will come true. It cannot fail the test of fulfillment and be a legitimate word from God. Words that come from God will illumine the future.

Finally, a true word from God is one that can be lived with. A revelation will bring encouragement and can survive an apparent literal disconformation. The author of Daniel, in the light of biblical archetypes, painted a portrait of what Antiochus IV stood for rather than giving a literal camera photograph of the tyrant. The Book of Daniel became a part of the Bible to give us perspective when we are up against a similar crisis.

Once again, we read that Daniel was left weak and lifeless from his talk with the heavenly being, and for the third time the angel encouraged him and by a touch got him on his feet again. Having strengthened Daniel to hear the dire divine revelation, the angel promised to return to take up the fight against "the prince of Persia" and the "prince of Greece" (10:18–20). In this struggle with the two nations, Michael, the patron angel of the Jews, was Gabriel's ally. The fortunes of the Jews were at stake in this angelic war, but the defeat of Persia and Greece was assured.

There Is More to History Than We Imagine

The Book of Daniel consistently affirms that heavenly powers share in the shaping of earthly history. The mention of Gabriel's and Michael's struggle with the unnamed leaders of Persia and Greece is just another way of emphasizing that truth. This implies several things. First, earthly rulers may delay and oppose God's purposes, but they cannot ultimately frustrate them. God is Lord on earth as well as in heaven.

Second, human actions do make a difference and human beings are responsible for history. Armies fight real battles, but the outcome is not the outworking of human decisions alone because something in the realm of the spirit lies behind them. Third, power has a dual nature. The leader of a powerful nation has a visible public human form, but that leader also personifies an invisible, immaterial driving spirit of a nation. Ancient kings in Daniel's time reflected their polytheistic gods; modern statesmen profile the "isms" that are the personalities of their countries—communism, fascism, etc. Fourth, earthly powers must inevitably come to terms with God their Creator.

The first six chapters of the Book of Daniel show how God used His spokesman to call world leaders back to their origin and destiny. The last six chapters (7–12) show how God dealt with nations that refused to acknowledge His reality. Daniel's prayer inaugurated war in heaven and opened up a way for God to confront political force with spiritual realities. The life of heaven is busier and more complex than we can imagine.

Finally, we discover in this scene that the plans of powerful nations do not always work out according to their blueprints. Imperial schemes are like a drunken cowboy—lift him in the saddle on one side of the horse and he will topple over on the other. There is more to history than we see, and what nations do is not always what they plan. Unexpected defeats and unexpected victories are commonplace, and the impossible does happen even in the smallest events of history.

For example, during the Second World War an American B-17 bomber, a Flying Fortress, flew when it was aerodynamically and technically impossible to do so. Actually, this particular B-17 flew out of Biskra on a bombing run to Tunisia. On its homeward flight it was attacked by German fighter planes, and an Me-109 closed in on its tail from above at the six o'clock position. The tail gunner on the B-17 killed the German pilot with a long burst of fire from his machine guns, but the fighter continued its dive and smashed into the tail section of the Fortress. The crash tore away the left horizontal stabilizer and elevator, and sliced the fuselage in half along a diagonal line running from the dorsal fin back and downward to the tail.

With this kind of damage it was theoretically impossible for the airplane to fly, but it flew for an hour and a half and made its way back to Biskra. Accompanying bomber crews stared in awe at the miracle unfolding before their eyes. The bomber negotiated a successful landing, but when a crewman opened a small hatch in the fuselage the airplane broke in half right there on the runway. The important thing, though, is that it made it home, even when there was no way that plane could fly. Whether big or small, historical events don't always go as planned, but all free human decisions, one way or another, unwittingly contribute to the working out of God's purpose. History is judged both *in* history and *above* history.

In this eleventh chapter of the Book of Daniel we have a long and detailed recital of events from Cyrus (538 B.C.) to the time of Antiochus IV (165 B.C.), who we position as the chief villain in every one of the dreams and visions. Like all apocalypses, the recital here is given in the form of a prediction, and as events get closer to 165 B.C. the scene gets more precise and vivid. Then when we come to the description in verse 40 covering events in the writer's own day, he peers into the unknown future with the grand assurance that God's judgment will strike the enemy of His people.

The Vision: History Unfolding (11:1–45)

At the beginning of our Scripture for this lesson the angel had promised to show Daniel the future (10:1). Now, in Chapter 11 Daniel gets a foreshortened view of history in one quick lesson in the guise of prediction (11:1–4). According to history, ten Persian kings succeeded Cyrus (538–529 B.C.). Among them were Cambyses (529–522 B.C.), Gaumata, who reigned for only seven months, Darius Hystaspis (522–485 B.C.), and Xerxes (485–465 B.C.), whose great expedition against Greece ended in disaster at Salamis (480 B.C.). Finally, the Persian Empire was conquered by Alexander the Great (336–323 B.C.) of Macedon in Greece. Alexander's early death brought about the four-part division of the Grecian empire. While none of these national leaders are mentioned by name in verses two through four of Chapter 11, their description helps us identify them.

From Cyrus to Alexander

To the modern reader it is no doubt puzzling that the Daniel author would devote such a little bit of space to the historic periods covered by the Persian and Greek empires. After all, the early kings of Persia were some of the most brilliant administrators in all of history, yet the Daniel author compresses the Persian period into one verse. And it was Alexander the Great and the Greek civilization that helped form the foundations of our Western culture, yet only two

How God Looks at History

verses in our story are devoted to this time. This serves to illustrate in living color that God's way of looking at greatness must be far different from ours.

It seems to me that the Daniel writer makes the point in Chapter 11 that secular history has no meaning in itself from God's perspective. This idea implies several things. First, it implies that secular history is going nowhere. It is nothing more than a meaningless sequence of power struggles that in the long run achieve nothing. Second, it becomes clear that the empires of Persia and Greece have no positive theological significance. However, when imperial powers use religion for their own political purposes, they provoke God to intervene to halt their consummate arrogance. Third, I believe we learn from this that history can have meaning if we look back upon it in the light of a revelation of God's eternal purposes. Indeed, God has revealed His purposes in the history of His chosen people, the Jews, and the kingdom of God. And the life, death, and resurrection of Jesus says that God lovingly cares for all people everywhere and wants to give meaning to their meaninglessness. And, finally, we learn from this that God will give meaning to all history by bringing it to an end—then His will will be done on earth as it is in heaven.

The Ptolemies of Egypt and the Seleucids of Syria

Our attention is next focused on the two kingdoms nearest Palestine—Egypt and Syria. The Jews were profoundly affected by these two neighbors who fought each other for sovereignty over Palestine. This history was well known to the writer of Daniel and his readers, and the kings described but not named are easily identified.

Ptolemy I (323–285 B.C.) was the king of the south who established a strong kingdom. Seleucus I (312–280 B.C.) was the king of the north, whose kingdom included Syria and Mesopotamia, who established an even greater kingdom (11:5). Ptolemy II (285–246 B.C.) made an alliance with the Seleucids by marrying his daughter, Bernice, to Antiochus II (261–247 B.C.). This angered Laodice, Antiochus' divorced first wife, and she conspired to have the royal couple and their son murdered (11:6). To avenge his sister Bernice,

Ptolemy III (246–221 B.C.) marched triumphantly against Seleucus II (246–227 B.C.), the son of Laodice. After a few years of warfare a truce was declared (11:7–9). All this "blood and gore" may be dull reading to us today, but it was intriguing to the Daniel writer and his readers because it set the stage for all their problems.

The writer then turned his attention to the shift in the balance of power under two sons of Seleucus II—Seleucus III (227–223 B.C.), and especially Antiochus III, the Great (223–187 B.C.). Antiochus III was at first successful in taking Palestine from Egypt, but Ptolemy IV (221–203 B.C.) counterattacked at Raphia in 217 B.C. (11:11–12). Finally Antiochus III overran Palestine by defeating the Egyptians at Gaza in 201 B.C. (11:13–15) and at Panias in 199 B.C. (11:16). To gain a stronger grip on Egypt, Antiochus III married his daughter Cleopatra to Ptolemy V. (Egypt had several Cleopatras, and this is not the woman of Julius Caesar, Mark Antony, and Hollywood film fame.)

This political move didn't work because Cleopatra championed Egypt and urged an alliance with Rome against Syria (11:17). When Antiochus III attempted to conquer Asia Minor and Greece, he was defeated by a Roman general at Magnesia in 190 B.C. On his way home he was killed when he tried to plunder a temple (11:18–19). Seleucus IV (187–175 B.C.) was assassinated by the very tax collector, Heliodorus, whom he had assigned to raise money to pay off the Roman debt after the battle of Magnesia (11:20).

The Wicked Career of Antiochus IV Epiphanes: A Forecast of the End Time

The Daniel author now brings into focus his main subject, Antiochus IV, the tyrant who in 165 B.C. was blaspheming God and murdering the Jews. We received a graphic description of Antiochus in the ram and the he-goat vision (Ch. 8), but here we are given at great length the sorry facts of his reign in the customary guise of prediction. The thrust of the vision at this point is that the wicked Antiochus is about to get his just deserts and that the End Time will soon bring relief to the suffering Jews. Both Antiochus's end and The End on God's calendar are at hand.

Daniel's message is that God has a way of dealing

with tyrants. For example, Napoleon seemed destined to conquer the world and exalted his own power in war. He sardonically commented that "God is always on the side of the heavy battalions." But eventually Napoleon was cut down to size and sent into exile. Victor Hugo the novelist remarked, "God got bored with him." Hugo also said that Napoleon was defeated at Waterloo not by Wellington alone but because "Napoleon had been denounced in the infinite and his fall had been decided on. He embarrassed God."

Antiochus, the "vile person" (11:21), pushed aside his brother Demetrius who legally had title to the throne, and by cunning and flattery gained power. He plotted the assassination of Jerusalem's High Priest Onias in 171 B.C. (11:22), and plundered the riches of Palestine at will (11:23–24). It looked as if nothing could stop him, but God had set a time limit on his program of destruction, and it would soon be over.

After the first campaign of Antiochus against Egypt (170 B.C.), he returned in triumph to Palestine. The Jews, hearing a rumor that he had been killed in Egypt, had declared their independence. As Antiochus assessed the scene, he decided their religion was at the heart of the trouble because the rebellious Jews had overthrown Menelaus, who had been forced upon them to replace Jason as High Priest. So the king initiated a bitter anti-Jewish program (11:25–28). We know that he plundered the Temple, slaughtered many of the people, garrisoned Syrian troops in Jerusalem, and put his hand-picked Menelaus back in office as High Priest. He held the erroneous belief that his kingdom could be made secure by violence.

A few months later Antiochus started his second campaign against Egypt (168 B.C.), but this time he suffered a defeat (11:29–30). He was frustrated by "the ships of Chittim," Roman vessels under the command of Popilius Lasenas. The Romans forced him back into Palestine in defeat. Antiochus had already shown his hostile attitude toward the faithful Jews, but on his homeward retreat to Syria he determined to destroy the Jewish religion altogether.

It was at this time that the acts of horror and desecration were committed that we already mentioned—he stationed troops in the Temple and set up an altar to the God Zeus in the sanctuary, the "transgression of desolation" of 8:13–14 (11:31). This was when he offered swine on the new altar, decreed an end to the Jewish religion, and dedicated the Jewish Temple to Zeus on the 25th of Kislev, 168 B.C. This story of infamy is told in 1 Maccabees 1 (in the Apocrypha), and is forever burned into the Jewish memory as an outrage that profaned the house of God.

The Use of Political Means to Accomplish Religious Purposes

Like a twentieth-century despot, Antiochus attacked the religion of his critics as subversive to his rule. Prophetic religion is always a threat to any totalitarian state, and when the lines are drawn God's faithful will stand firm. At this time the Jews were divided into two parties, the Hellenizers who betrayed the covenant, and the *Hasidim* who remained firm under persecution (11:32–35). The wise Jews, like Daniel and the *Hasidim,* stood their ground and took action against Antiochus. We don't know whether this action was in the form of a quiet withdrawal or a belligerent armed revolt as epitomized by the Maccabees.

As the Jewish martyrs began to fall, the Maccabean revolt was started by Mattathias in Modein in 168 B.C. This romantic and successful revolution for a brilliant moment saved the Jews from Antiochus and his foreign rule. The author of Daniel called this armed revolt "a little help," so he could not have expected much from it (11:34). He doesn't seem to be against the use of force in winning or maintaining religious freedom, but he doesn't appear to have great confidence in it either. He knew that justice delayed might be justice denied, but he seemed to sense that returning violence for violence only multiplied violence. For him the battle with Antiochus was a spiritual warfare and ultimately would be settled by the power of God's character rather than by the swords of the Maccabees.

Faithful Christians still agonize in conscience today over using force to preserve human rights, and we may never find the perfect theoretical formulae that will settle every moral problem involved. For one Christian, submission, suffering, and martyrdom is the only response to persecution, while for another Christian, armed resistance is the acceptable route. For the author of Daniel, the martyrdom of the saintly leaders purged the community of the faithful. Most of us don't know how much we believe in something until its truth or falsity becomes a matter of life or death for us. But noncooperation with evil is as much a duty as is cooperation with good. For the Christian, the death of Christ purges the sins of the whole world (Rom. 3:23–25; 5:12, 18).

The King Who Asserted Himself: Antiochus Played God

The Daniel writer next exposes the further arrogance of the king as he exalted himself to the godhead, disregarded all gods but Zeus, and assigned rewards to his partisans (11:36–39). Like most tyrants, Antiochus couldn't resist the temptation to play at being God, weaving religion into his political schemes. He needed to unify his kingdom around loyalty to himself "for reasons of national security," so all the local deities had to go including the God of the Jews. He therefore set himself above every god by taking the title Epiphanes (God manifest), and honored only the Olympian Zeus, a Greek deity strange even to his own Syrian subjects. He made use of the god of war ("the god of forces") for his own brutal conquests, but he respected only his own superiority. This was a provocation to which God had to respond, and it heralded the End Time.

Whenever human leaders try to play God they become devils. Over the last thirty-five hundred years of history self-exalted leaders have given us only one hundred and sixty-eight years without war. Our twentieth century has been the cruelest as we have watched "divine" dictators enslave and slaughter millions. Their arrogance has been a blasphemy against God as they put their final trust in their own ability to wage war. Their "godhead" has been Satanic, and they have robbed their subjects of human dignity. From 1775 to the present, the United States of America alone has suffered approximately 2,375,-546 casualties in war.

The Jews were as shocked at Antiochus as we have been shocked at our own homegrown dictators. Such blasphemous presumption is short-lived in any century. Just as God dethroned Nebuchadnezzar so He would pull Antiochus's divine status out from under him. Every act of self-magnification carries the seeds of its own defeat—in the long run, evil destroys itself. Nations and kings are not necessarily evil, but they do have an irresistible tendency to worship themselves.

The End Time for Antiochus

So far the Daniel author has been looking back over his shoulder and reciting the facts of recent history with measurable accuracy. Now he comes to the moment when he describes the present—the last phase and the fall of Antiochus IV. From this point he will predict the future with the perfect assurance that the tyrant would soon fall and the drama would end (11:40–45). He peered into the future and foresaw that the king of Egypt would attack Antiochus, but that Antiochus would counterattack and win a decisive victory. On his way through Palestine, Antiochus would slaughter tens of thousands of the faithful Jews, but he bypassed those partisans who had sold out to him. At the peak of his conquest he would hear alarming news from his home country in the east and north (11:44) and, as a result, he would dash home in a fury to meet the threat there.

The Daniel writer knew the end for the vicious Antiochus was near and saw it coming "between the seas" and "the glorious holy mountain" (11:45). Various interpretations have been given of this prediction. But we know for sure that Antiochus marched east in the spring of 165 B.C. to guard his frontiers against the threat of the Parthians. Months later he developed mental illness and died a mysterious death at Tabae in Persia. When the author was writing the Book of Daniel these events had not taken place, but in a general way he was able to sketch the coming months.

Antiochus was on the verge of world dominion when trouble in the east stopped him dead in his tracks. This was the beginning of the End Time. We see now as we have before that God still directed history, that God's purpose for His people was about to be fulfilled, that the reader of the Book of Daniel could have confidence in the prevailing power of God, and that the kingdoms of this world will be replaced by the kingdom of God. One thing is certain. In spite of the varied datings and interpretations of this marvelous Book of Daniel, all Bible students are agreed that the spotlight is focused throughout on the kingdom of God!

God Is in Control

Throughout the Book of Daniel the author affirms that God is in control of the events of Jewish history. This implies several things. First, God does give His people free will, and they are responsible to Him and to themselves for their destiny. He even did the same for pagan kings such as Nebuchadnezzar and Belshazzar (Dan. 4–5). We see clearly that God's people must choose to walk in His way; they are never forced to do so. Believers are not like toy soldiers with an imposed destiny.

Second, I believe the author of Daniel used the literary device of writing past history as if it were "pre-written." This was his way of affirming that God was in control of the details of Israel's history. It was an apocalyptic style of writing and was neither history written in advance nor prophecy after the event. This "prewritten" history went beyond history and provided a timeless revelation for the first century B.C., the first century A.D., and for any century in the future to the ultimate end of time as we know it.

Third, we see that no one can frustrate God's ultimate purpose in history for His people. God will finally defeat evil and establish His rule in the world. God is determined to achieve His righteous reign, and He will. Daniel expected this heavenly kingdom to appear in the near future, but his portrayal of the End Time is an imaginative scenario rather than a forecast of precisely how things must be.

The Epilogue: The Final Consummation (12:1–13)

In the first four verses of Chapter 12 the writer anticipated an end to the persecution in the future and the beginning of the kingdom of God. In the rest of Chapter 12 Daniel foresaw in his vision that time when the end would come (12:11). There were definite limits placed on those who opposed God.

As we see it, while the author of Daniel was writing his book, Antiochus was still alive, the faithful Jews were still losing their lives, and the Temple still housed the statue of the god Zeus. Now, the author's readers are warned that bitter days lie ahead, "and there shall be a time of trouble such as never was" (12:1). Next, though, came the assurance that "at that time thy people shall be delivered, every one that shall be found written in the book."

The Climax of Wrath

Michael, the patron angel of the Jews, we're told, would see to it that the true keepers of God's covenant would be delivered. While the believer-saints would suffer, ultimately the kingdom of God would be delivered into their hands. Since triumph came through tribulation, the prospect of violent death was no surprise to the faithful people of God, but the End Time had actually arrived. The demonic Antiochus IV had failed to realize that behind the Temple and the Jewish people stood God, the Almighty One, and that as the embodiment of godless wickedness, Antiochus was about to suffer a final defeat. So the author's portrait of Antiochus's end is not a failed attempt to give a literal account of his death, but a true promise that God would make an end of his despotism.

Early in this part of our Scripture lesson we have one of the most remarkable passages in the Old Testament for the growing belief in life after death. The angel said to Daniel, "And many of them that sleep in the dust of the earth shall awake, some to everlasting life, and some to shame and everlasting contempt" (12:2). The general concept of existence after death in Judaism was hazy, gloomy, and full of despair. In early Old Testament times the Israelites believed they lived on through their children and grandchildren. They had no hope of individual survival beyond the grave. Sheol, or the Pit, a subterranean cavern underneath the earth, was the destiny of

The Promise of Life: The Secure Destiny of the Faithful—and the Wicked

all people. At death a person's "shade" went to Sheol, a land of no return, where only a shadowy replica of the once living person endured.

In a few places the hope is expressed that God will keep His people from entering Sheol (Psa. 16:8–11) or that God will raise them again to life (Isa. 26:19). But here in verse 2 we have three new ideas added to these earlier teachings of a resurrection from the dead: first, the resurrection of the wicked, which is taught here for the first time; second, the idea of rewards and punishment in the afterlife; and third, not all will be raised—a general resurrection of everyone doesn't appear to be seen by the wording of the verse, though interpreters differ as to the explicit meaning.

A Hope of Life after Death for the Martyrs

The Book of Daniel, then, teaches a resounding hope in the ultimate resurrection of the dead. This implies several things. First, God will see to it that the destiny of faithful people is secure. Truth and commitment will be vindicated in a life after life. Second, God guarantees that those martyred for their faith will not lose their share in the life, glory, and joy of God's people. Those who believe in God never see each other for the last time.

Third, we get the implication that the resurrection is not an individual experience but is corporate in character. A person has new life as a social part of the family of God. New life is given to individuals, but not to them individually. Fourth, new life is a gift of God. We are not naturally immortal, so God must raise us from the dead. We are recalled to life as a full personality by a new creative act of God. Fifth, the wicked are also judged and punished. And sixth, the implications found in verse 2 fall short of the Christian expectation and the hope that come from Christ's resurrection from the dead. Daniel helped prepare the way for Christ, but the Christian's hope looks to a personal life with God after this life, a life of complete fulfillment, joy, and growth in character. Evangelist Billy Graham has often said, "For the Christian, the grave is not the end; nor is death a calamity, for he has a glorious hope—the hope of heaven."

Gabriel also told Daniel that the "wise shall shine as the brightness of the firmament; and they that turn many to righteousness as the stars for ever and ever" (12:3). This meant that wise men like Daniel, whose teaching had been so often despised and rejected, would have their situation reversed and be given a position of preeminent honor. Daniel-like people would be held in high regard by God while Antiochus-like people would end up in disrepute and abhorrence. The discerning and faithful people who had already come to grips with suffering and shame would rise from the dust to an inheritance of lasting life, but Antiochus, in his vainglorious arrogance, would be doomed to eternal disgrace.

Gabriel then told Daniel to "shut up the words, and seal the book, even to the time of the end" (12:4). This presumedly referred to the entire Book of Daniel which was to remain sealed until the End Time. Only then were these words to be disclosed. This common apocalyptic device of sealing pseudonymous books until their time of fulfillment was at hand was meant to encourage the faithful to hang on just a little longer.

The Wise Will Also Share in Eternal Life

Throughout the Book of Daniel the faithful people of God are challenged to steadfastness. This implies several things. First, Daniel is held up as a model of leadership. Daniel-like behavior—faithfulness to God and His Law—is what both leaders and people should emulate. The discerning believer is encouraged to be as steadfast in his loyalty as Daniel was. Second, it implies that Daniel was a wise teacher, and faithful religious teachers are to pass on to their listeners and readers what they believe God is revealing about the past, present, and future, and to encourage them not to cooperate with the Antiochus-like unbelievers. Third, we are to see that information can help people make up their minds about issues and influence their behavior in a positive direction. God's written Word is just as much a revelation as His spoken word, and it can be applied both in the present and in the future. And fourth, the suffering of

The Call to Be Courageous

faithful people can have a positive significance. It is not a means of provoking God to come to the rescue of His people, but it can have a refining effect on the community of the faithful. It can force people to make up their mind about which side they are on, and make them wary of depending too heavily on physical violence to achieve their spiritual goals. The faithful Jews' love for God made their death a martyrdom rather than a mere execution.

The Last Message to Daniel

We have now come to the last scene in the Book of Daniel. Daniel and Gabriel were still by the Tigris river (10:5), and on either side of the river there was another angelic figure. Once again Daniel wanted to know (see 7:25) how long the suffering under Antiochus would last. Then Gabriel, with both hands raised toward heaven, swore that the End would come after three and a half set periods (12:5–7). As soon as the tyrant Antiochus was dead all would be over.

Like us, Daniel found this answer more puzzling than illuminating, so he asked for some clarification. When he tried the question again he was told to let the matter rest "for the words are closed up and sealed till the time of the end" (12:9). Meanwhile the struggle with Antiochus would go on and more of the faithful Jews would even be martyred. But purity and cleansing would come to those who held out to the death. Antiochus and the other wicked ones would continue in their ignorant evil because they had no understanding of why believers would rather die than compromise their faith. Those with Daniel-like wisdom and faith would know that the martyrs weren't throwing their lives away because a life dedicated to God is never wasted (12:10).

In verses 11 and 12 we are given a different set of figures used in calculation of the End Time—1,335 days. This may be accounted for by the fact that various calendars were in use in the second century B.C., and the question of a right calendar was a matter of dispute. The Babylonians used a lunar calendar (354 days), the Greeks followed a lunar-solar calendar (360 days), and the Essenes used a solar calendar (364 days). It is possible the period of days used by the Daniel writer is related to all three calendars because his readers were using more than one calendar. The important point being made is that the End Time had been set by God. The assurance was given that the terrible tribulation through which they had been suffering would soon be over. There was hope ahead!

Then comes the final word of assurance, "But go thou thy way till the end be: for thou shalt rest, and stand in thy lot at the end of the days" (12:13). In other words, Daniel was told to carry on his normal activities because the future was in the hands of God. In due time Daniel would die like everyone else, but death would not be the final word on him. At the End Time God would raise him from the grave to stand in his allotted place to see the New Age ushered in. This was a promise of great beauty and power to Daniel and the readers of the book, and this promise was expanded into a major theme by the New Testament writers.

In what sense did the End Time come for the author of Daniel? If the writer lived for a few years longer, he saw the elimination of Antiochus, the cleansing of the Temple, the national independence of the Jews, and the Maccabees installed as religious and political rulers of the nation. But if he lived for several more decades he saw things continue about as they had been before, especially as the Maccabean dynasty became more and more corrupt and oppressive. He would have realized that the promise of the ultimate realization of God's kingship had been partially fulfilled, but partially unfulfilled. He knew that God's kingship couldn't be just nationalistic, individualistic, mystical, or humanly generated—others had tried these routes only to fail. He would have realized that because the End Time had come in part in his day, it would come completely in a future day.

A little over a century and a half later the angel Gabriel again appeared, as in Daniel 9, and began a chain of events that led to the birth of Jesus (Luke 1). Jesus ushered in the End Time that Daniel had promised, and the "son of man" figure of Daniel 7 provided a key image by which Jesus described Himself. Jesus, like Daniel, accepted the suffering of the

When Comes the End Time? The New Testament and Later

people of God as a part of His ministry (Mark 8:31), and agreed with Daniel that He came to serve rather than to be served (Mark 10:45). When Jesus began to describe the End Time that was still to come (Mark 13), He used Daniel's language of troubling rumors, persecution, falling away, courage to endure, deliverance of the faithful, and the coming of the Son of man in clouds with great power and glory.

The Apostle Paul also used the language of Daniel to describe the End Time when he spoke of people rising from the dead (1 Thess. 4, 5; 1 Cor. 15); the Apostle's picture of the "lawless man" (2 Thess. 2) reflects Daniel's portrait of Antiochus IV. The Book of Revelation, facing a similar pressure situation as that which existed under Antiochus, took over wholesale the phraseology and imagery of Daniel. Chapter after chapter in the Book of Revelation is based upon the structure and content of the Book of Daniel. And when the Revelation writer applied the scheme of empires in Daniel to his own day (as one example), he was applying the visions of Daniel as they should be applied.

Daniel in Our Day

As we move toward the close of the twentieth century and look ahead to the twenty-first century, it is quite legitimate to reapply the visions of Daniel in the same way the New Testament did. Daniel's vision of empires included Babylon, Persia, Greece, and the Seleucids; his visions could just as easily include Rome, Islam, Britain, Germany, Russia, America, or Israel. The genius of Daniel's symbols is that they are gifts of God to be reapplied as the same dark forces of international history drive nations to try to play God. Antiochus-like leaders are alive and well in our nuclear age, a time in which we have invented the power to destroy ourselves and the world in which we live. God began our story, but He has allowed us to discover a way to end it. We can speed the End Time, or we can delay it—Daniel's visions are a reality and quite appropriate for our time.

Daniel has remained through the centuries a favorite book of the Bible, and rightly so. The Maccabeean revolution and the reading of the Book of

Daniel kept the Jewish faith alive in 165 B.C. It served the Jews in the emergency of the Roman war of A.D. 68–70, and proved indispensable to the Christians under Caesar Domitian's persecution around A.D. 95. It is still a classic in our time, and we can turn to it again and again with profit.

Daniel portrays God as powerful, sovereign, and almighty—a personal God who hears prayers, who suddenly appears at Nebuchadnezzar's furnace, and in the lions' den, who helps us to escape fires but may allow us to perish in fires, who controls events, and who can reveal to us the meaning of history. Lasting dominion belongs to Daniel's God, and He can use even dumb and evil rulers to bring about His wishes.

God is so gracious that He helps the faithful believer live with history even when we cannot control history. Daniel's God is an international God who challenges His faithful followers to be involved in present politics on the one hand and to view all history from the End Time on the other hand. Daniel invites us to live our lives in the presence of his God with both political commitment and religious faithfulness.

Sir Walter Scott, the novelist, had a library stacked from floor to ceiling with thousands of volumes. When he was near death he asked one of his servants to read to him. "What shall I read?" the man asked. "The Bible," Scott said. "Nothing else will give you comfort when you lie here." To all who are weary and seek rest; to all who mourn and long for comfort; to all who struggle and desire victory; to all who sin and need a Savior; to all who are idle and look for service; to all who are strangers and want fellowship; to all who hunger and thirst after righteousness; and to whosoever will, come and read—the Book of Daniel opens wide its pages to you in the name of Jesus Christ its Lord.

Holy Lord, Thank You for the times You've been with me in my own lions' dens, in my own fiery furnaces. Each time You've delivered me in Your own way and timing. Thank You for being so good to me. AMEN.

197

WHAT THIS SCRIPTURE MEANS TO ME
Daniel 10–12

During the month of December, the pace of life seems to quicken dramatically. As the Christmas holiday approaches, each day is marked by a flurry of activity which seems to accelerate as December 25 gets closer. Gifts are bought, wrapped and mailed; traditional meals are prepared; and numerous social and religious functions are attended. In spite of attempts to remain calm and peaceful, the Advent and Christmas seasons often seem chaotic, hectic, and out of control.

This past year, I tried something new. I made a decision to enjoy some good old-fashioned "R and R"—rest and relaxation—once each day. The time I set for myself was four o'clock in the afternoon when the mail arrived. While our son watched *Sesame Street* on TV, I made myself some coffee or hot cocoa and retreated to the back room with the stack of cards, letters, bills, papers, or whatever else had been placed in our mailbox. While sipping my warm, delicious drink, I would slowly and carefully read the messages people had written in Christmas cards or newsletters. In many cases, these holiday greetings are the only source of information I receive about some of my friends. They are the once-a-year correspondences that enable us to keep in touch regardless of the passage of time or the distance between us.

One afternoon at four, I noticed a familiar return address on a bright red envelope in the mailbox. The card was from a longtime friend. I knew from past experience that I was in for a treat. My friend's letters always contained lots of news about people I knew as well as detailed accounts of her family's activities.

Once settled in my quiet place, with a mug of steaming coffee in hand, I opened the envelope and removed the Christmas card. But as I began reading her handwritten note, the words sounded strange: "We've had so many ups and downs this year. . . . My husband's health hasn't been good. . . . All of the test results aren't in yet. . . . We've had to change some of our holiday plans."

I felt my heart beating faster and the pace of my reading increase dramatically. Surely she would tell me what was happening, describe the symptoms, or *somehow* explain her suspicions. I quickly glanced through the remaining page to read her "bottom line." I couldn't believe it—her only conclusion was, "Pray for us. We need it." I sat motionless, trying to make some sense out of her sketchy details. More and more questions came to mind, for which there were no answers.

In some ways I think Daniel might have experienced some of these feelings following his final vision. He asked, "How long shall it be till the end of these wonders?" (12:6, RSV). We learn that he heard the response, but did not understand it (12:8). His second question, "What shall be the issue of these things?" (12:8, RSV) was never directly answered.

Unfortunately, life is full of uncertainty. There are many unanswered questions, many areas of misunderstanding. We can't expect to interpret correctly all of the events or situations which occur. But in spite of the difficulties we face, Daniel encourages us to have faith, and to trust in God's goodness and mercy, and above all, His promise to preserve and protect all who remain faithful to His covenant.

Index

The Guideposts Bible Study Program is published by the same people who publish *Guideposts*—a monthly inspirational magazine filled with faith-filled stories. Subscribing to *Guideposts* is easy. All you have to do is write Guideposts Associates, Inc., 39 Seminary Hill Road, Carmel, New York 10512. A year's subscription costs only $8.95 in the United States, and $10.95 in Canada and overseas. Our Big Print edition, for those with special reading needs, is only $8.95 in the United States, Canada and abroad.